A PURPLE HEART STORY

A PURPLE HEART STORY

*My Experiences in the US Army
and the Korean War*

DONALD R. SONSALLA, PhD

Michelle
I hope you enjoy the
ramblings of an old
veteran

Dr. Sonsalla

A Purple Heart Story
My Experiences in the US Army
and the Korean War

ISBN 978-0-615-71150-8

DEDICATION

To my family, the members of the military and especially my foxhole buddies from B Company, Fifteenth Regiment, Third Infantry Division, US Army Korea 1950–53.

CONTENTS

INTRODUCTION

"Old men make wars and young men die." I don't know who said it, but I remember this line from an old TV episode of *MASH*. It comes to mind as I write this story for my children and grandchildren about my experiences in the Korean War.

I Served with Heroes

I was fortunate to serve with the bravest soldiers from all parts of the world. As an infantry soldier in Baker Company, I met combat buddies from the West, the East, the North, the South, and all places in between. Even though we were from different places and had different religious beliefs, we had one thing in common. We were willing to face the enemy and give our lives for each other. We established a bond that could never be broken nor understood by others.

We merged into one fighting entity.

Yes, we killed, and we conquered hill after hill and fought the elements as well as the enemy. We endured the extreme cold, the snowstorms, the endless climbing of mountains, the constant barrage of gunfire, and the loss of friends. We met in foxholes, became dear friends, and lost each other to a bullet, a grenade, or a bomb.

With each battle the casualty count mounted, as friends fell by the wayside. I lamented their loss, cried "Why them?" and then my time came and I fell wounded. Others who carried on told me I was lucky to make it out alive. I watched them go off and fight again, and I felt frustration because I couldn't go with them—I could no longer continue the fight.

Ground combat cannot be explained or understood by those who have not lived through it. The acrid smell of explosives; the crump, crump, crump of mortar and

1

artillery fire; the staccato sound of automatic fire; the whining, whizzing, and flapping, never-to-be-forgotten sound of careening fragments; the frozen cry of a dying soldier; the screams of the wounded; and the smell of warm blood, burning bodies, and spilled guts. Foul memories indeed! At night, the horror is magnified and intensified by the strobe-like flashes from the rifle fire and the tracers waving like mystical wands seemingly at arm's length.

The bleached-out pasty white faces of the frightened and wounded are engraved in my mind's eye forever. The soldier clutching a wound, the boy calling his mother, the silent moving mouth will never be forgotten. Prayers are not answered, and men die. "Why?" I asked. "Why?"

The extreme cold, the rain, and the snow; the wet, the dirt, and the filth; the hunger; the thirst; and the physical exhaustion that nearly breaks you—these are the bit players accompanying the soldier in his daily quest for survival. Combat takes place in the worst weather, at the worst time of day (night), in the worst of terrain, and accompanied by the worst smells and sounds. You never forget the sulfuric smell of death. The stench of unburied, decomposing bodies fills the air, choking your lungs and imprinting the odor in your mind forever. Bodies and parts of bodies are strewn over the battlefield. Bodies of your friends and the enemy are intertwined on the battle-scarred ground. There is no time to think: the bullets and shells are headed in your direction. Your mind screams to kill those bastards. You forget any fear of death. You have one thought: do unto them as they did to your foxhole buddies.

You relish the thought of total destruction of the enemy. You forget all body pain; your body is constantly pumping adrenaline. Your eardrums almost burst from the noise, and your arms and fingers are tired from the constant firing of your weapon. No matter how many enemies you kill, they keep coming up the hill. There seems to be no end. The question in your mind keeps playing over and over. Who will run out of ammunition first—you or the enemy? Luckily, the Chinese and North Koreans ran out first.

The bond of brotherhood is hard to explain. You live, breath, joke, and share the greatest of gifts with your foxhole buddies: *the gift of your life*. There was never a question in my mind that I was willing to die for my foxhole buddies, and they, in turn, were willing to die for me.

Recorded in this book are some of my combat experiences as an infantryman during the Korean War from November 11, 1950, to March 24, 1951. More happens in a minute of combat than happens in a year as a civilian. In your foxhole, you have a front row seat to the spectacle of war—you can touch, smell, taste, see, feel, and experience combat.

This book is based on my memories and my research of the Korean War via videotapes, books, magazine articles, and the Internet. At annual reunions, I talked to fellow Baker Company veterans, who helped me recall things I had worked so hard to forget.

I have supplemented this story with pictures from various sources to help the reader better understand the Korean War. I decided to take that history and interweave my own recollections as little vignettes. But as I wrote, the memories flooded back like a downpour sometimes causing pain and sleepless nights. Sometimes I may be too graphic and describe horrible things, but WAR IS HORRIBLE.

When I went to Washington, DC, for the Korean War Memorial dedication, I stared into those stark cold statue faces frozen in agony. They reminded me of the frozen faces I'd seen, lit up by flares during the war. The Korean War was publicized as the forgotten war, but those of us who experienced it can never forget.

The memories of a war more than sixty years ago lurk in the not-forgotten experiences of my life, no matter how hard I try to forget. Memories emerge during quiet times or when a sight, smell, or sound signals the soul to recall. Then the mind spews forth, in spits and starts, long-ago thoughts—some happy, some sad, some terrible.

When I think of war, and those days so long ago, I agonize over my guilt for killing and ask, "Was I really like that?" And I suffer the guilt of being a survivor, "Why did I live and my buddies die?" These questions will haunt me forever.

After I left Korea, I buried those thoughts, and they remained deep inside me except for an occasional flashback. Thankfully, time in its own way submerges the dark and foul and replaces it with newer, sweeter, and better memories. The sound of a baby's call, the soft words of a lover's voice, the laughter of friends and children—these are the thoughts I treasure now, the monuments to good living and finding peace within one's self. As life progressed, I went to school, met a fantastic woman, got married, had two wonderful daughters, and acquired two sons-in-law and four grandchildren.

The Korean Peninsula. Long known as the "Hermit Kingdom," Korea was little known to the outside world prior to 1950. In 1910, the troops of Imperial Japan occupied the Korean Peninsula despite the resistance of the Korean people. The Allied powers promised Korea its independence in 1943, once Japan was defeated. However, in 1945, the Japanese forces south of the 38th Parallel surrendered to the Americans while those in the north capitulated to the Soviet Russians. The border between the two Koreas took on increased importance in August 1948 when the American supported government in the south formed the "Republic of Korea." Its first president, Syngman Rhee governed over 21 million Koreans in the south but also proclaimed sovereignty over the entire country. Within a month the Communist "Democratic Republic of Korea" was formed by President Kim Il-Sung north of the 38th Parallel. His republic, with a population of nine million, also claimed to be the rightful government of all the Korean people. The stage was thus set for conflict.

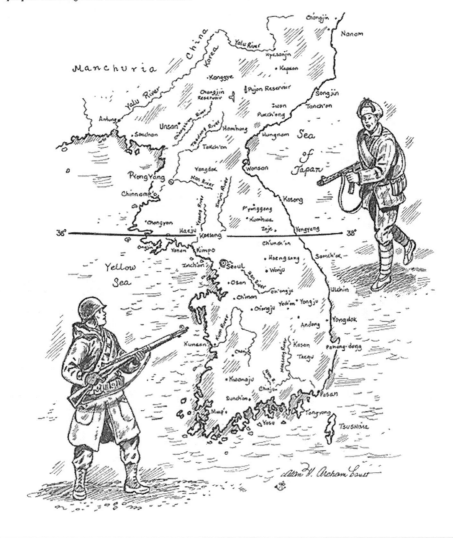

CHAPTER ONE

REMEMBERING THE KOREAN WAR, SIXTY YEARS AGO

You haven't lived until you've almost died. After you experience combat, everything else is anticlimactic. This is a story about my role in the Korean War. It has been more than sixty years since the beginning of the Korean War in 1950. After decades of Japanese occupation, Korea was divided in half at the 38th parallel by Allied Forces at the end of World War II, with the south part administered by the United States and the north part by Soviet Russia. Deep divisions built over several years, leading to skirmishes and finally an invasion of South Korea by North Korean troops on June 25, 1950, later augmented by more than two hundred thousand Chinese troops in December 1950.

The United Nations sent troops and support from twenty-one countries to help South Korea; those soldiers were primarily from the United States and Britain. The war lasted for three years, with large advances and retreats on both sides and many casualties. Hundreds of thousands of civilians and soldiers were killed. The United States reported 53,686 killed in action (KIA); 92,134 wounded in action (WIA); and 4,759 missing in action (MIA). The two Koreas are technically still at war since hostilities ended in a ceasefire—not a peace treaty—at the 38th parallel in 1953.

Though it is often referred to as "The Forgotten War," I hope my story and collection of photographs helps us to remember the events of 1950–1953, the people involved, and the legacy that still remains, sixty years later. I am a part of that legacy. I served two years, two months, and twenty-four days as a US soldier. I was willing to fight for freedom, and as John Quincy Adams said, "Posterity—you will never know how much it cost my generation to preserve your freedom. I hope you make good use of it." Make good use of my service; enjoy the story and the ramblings of an old veteran.

CHAPTER TWO

CIVILIAN TO SOLDIER

I graduated from Cotter, an all-boys high school in Winona, Minnesota, in June 1949. Cotter was next door to Cathedral, an all-girls high school. We spent a lot of time by the windows giving signals to the girls, and they in turn signaled us. One time I got in trouble by holding a small kid (Virgil, who later became a priest in the town where my wife, Verna, was raised) out the window by his feet from the second floor. My nickname in high school was Suds (maybe a relation to beer suds). There was soap on the market at the time called "Super Suds." Whenever I played football (I was starting lineman for three years) and was sent into the game or came out of the game, the cheerleaders performed a special cheer—the jingle for "Super Suds."

Super Suds. Super Suds
Lots more suds from Super Suds.

Cotter High School (left) consisted of grades 9–12 with a graduating class of forty in 1949. Next to Cotter High School was a recreation center.

I started driving a semi-truck for the Madison Silo Company when I was a sophomore in high school, delivering eighty-pound cement silo blocks to farmers in Minnesota, Wisconsin, and Iowa as well as North and South Dakota. During the summer, it was a full-time job and a good source of income.

After graduation from high school, I continued to drive a semi-truck for Madison Silo. I enjoyed the job and, at the time, thought this would be my career. My dad worked for Madison Silo, and we took many trips together. He was a strong man, a hard worker, and we had a friendly unspoken competition to see who could load or unload the cement blocks the fastest. I enjoyed the camaraderie of working with my father.

My dad, Robert Sonsalla, drove one of these semi-trucks used for hauling cement silo blocks. I also drove the trucks while in high school, college, and several summers after I was married. I enjoyed driving and the opportunity to see the countryside.

I had received letters from some local colleges regarding a football scholarship. I really did not have any plans to attend college, since I was working at a good job and making a lot of money. I was a big, strong kid—six feet tall and weighing two hundred and sixty pounds with a lot of muscle from lifting cement blocks. Max Molock, the football coach at St. Mary's College, and John Nett, my high school coach, came to my house one night. They had my high school grades and test scores, and Max offered me a full scholarship to attend St. Mary's College, a small liberal arts Catholic college in Winona, Minnesota, if I would play football. I agreed to play football if I could continue to drive a truck.

In the fall of 1949, I was working part-time as a truck driver and attending St. Mary's College on a football scholarship. I enrolled in a liberal arts program and carried a full load, which required a lot of reading. At St. Mary's College, I was starting offensive and defensive guard on the football team. In 1949, football players played both defensive and offensive positions. I started in all of the games and played almost the entire game.

I recall one game against St. Thomas College, where I made a tackle and my fingers got caught in the shoulder pads of the fullback slashing through the line. I split my hand open. There was blood all over. I came over to the bench, and Coach Molock, a tough Polock just like me, looked at the hand, taped it up, gave me a shot of Novocain, and sent me in to finish the game. After the game, I went to the hospital and got several stitches. I still have the scar as a memory of my gridiron activities.

I attended one semester at St. Mary's College. I was not an academically motivated student at that time, and after football season was over, I reassessed my future. I knew I was seeking something other than driving a truck or going to school, but I didn't know what it was. I had received passing grades but really had no interest in continuing college. So rather than return to St. Mary's for the second semester, in March 1950, at the age of nineteen, I enlisted in the US Army seeking a new adventure.

I raised my right hand and swore allegiance to the United States at the Winona Courthouse.

> *"I, Donald R. Sonsalla, do solemnly swear that I will support and defend the Constitution of the United States against all enemies, foreign and domestic; that I will bear true faith and allegiance to the same; and that I will obey the orders of the President of the United States and the orders of the officers appointed over me, according to regulations and the Uniform Code of Military Justice. So help me God."*

9

With this oath, I became a soldier.

After enlisting in the Army, I boarded a train in Winona with three other enlisted soldiers (or recruits). We traveled together with orders to report to Fort Ord, California. I was excited because I had never been to California. As we traveled west, I took in the scenery from the windows of the train. One highlight was traveling on the bridge over the Great Salt Lake. Every time the train stopped at a station for a short time, we ran into town to the nearest joint and bought some beer because beer on the train was expensive.

I arrived at Fort Ord, California. The weather was nice, and I saw the Pacific Ocean for the first time. I reported to the base and was assigned to a Fourth Division basic training outfit. While growing up in Winona, one of my favorite games was playing soldier. I had several toy forts, lead soldiers, toy guns, and an O gauge military railroad train. Little did I know that in a few years I would ride on a real train, live in a real fort, and trade in my toy gun for a real gun.

Donald R. Sonsalla, above, son of Mr. and Mrs. Robert Sonsalla, 115 East Fifth street, enlisted in the regular Army Tuesday for two years and is taking his basic training at Fort Ord, Calif. He is a graduate of Cotter High school where for three years he played guard on the football team. He had been a student at St. Mary's college prior to his enlistment.

My basic training company consisted of previous service members, called retreads, who had been discharged and then reenlisted. They had served in the Air Force, Navy, and Marines as well as the Army, and because of previous service, some had earned several stripes. (Stripes designated rank.) I was a recruit and had no stripes. Because our group included these former military personnel, our training company was quickly moved to advanced commando tactics.

During basic training, we put in long hours and relished any break. You learn to appreciate small things under such conditions. During the first couple of weeks, we were restricted to company grounds and could not leave the area, but because of the large number of retreads in our company (about 50 percent), that restriction was lifted after two weeks. My first venture was to go shopping at the PX (Post Exchange). My second venture was the Post Library, where I found refuge in books and newspapers.

In the evenings, we were free to enjoy the beer hall. Our tough old drill sergeant with the deep voice marched us there. Even though he had a heart of gold, I was afraid of him. He was six feet tall and had many medals. To get to the beer hall, we had to cross over a highway on a bridge. We were told to use route step, not cadence step marching, because if a large group marched in cadence on a bridge, it could cause the bridge to weaken and possibly fall down.

I was housed in a large, wooden barrack that accommodated thirty to forty bunks in a row. There was a group shower room and bathroom at one end of the barracks and the top sergeant's room at the other end. We each had a footlocker at the end of our bunk. We were responsible for keeping our footlocker in neat shape and our bunk crisply made; you never knew when the sergeant would come in during daily inspection and bounce a quarter on your bunk.

Early every morning we had a spit and polish inspection. When I first got to basic, we were issued GI clothes and received a buzz haircut (heiney). We learned how to shine shoes. We were given combat boots that were raw leather, and we had to put polish on them and make them shine. One of the secrets to get a good shine was to put polish on the boot and then set it on fire. It melted the shoe polish right into the leather. I can still recall a bunch of kids sitting out on the street in front of the barracks burning their boots and laughing. It seems laughter was good medicine in the Army. I enjoyed the camaraderie of my fellow soldiers.

We had classes and heard lectures about the proud history of the US Army. We memorized the Soldier's Creed:

I am an American soldier.
I am a warrior and a member of a team.
I serve the people of the United States and live the Army values.
I will always place the mission first.
I will never accept defeat.
I will never quit.
I will never leave a fallen comrade.
I am disciplined, physically and mentally tough,
Trained and proficient in my warrior tasks and drills.
I always maintain my arms, my equipment, and myself.
I am an expert, and I am a professional.
I stand ready to deploy, engage, and destroy the enemies of the United
*   States of America in close combat.*
I am a guardian of freedom and the American way of life.
I am an American soldier."

Basic Training

Posing and cleaning guns in front of our barracks at Fort Ord in California.

Basic Training

Sometimes basic training seemed like jail. Still, there was a lot of clowning around.

Basic Training

Often basic training was work on the obstacle course (below) and firing range. I was used to handling a rifle since I did a lot of hunting in Winona.

Mess hall at Ford Ord, where I had my first taste of SOS and honeydew melon.

Some of the highlights of basic training:

- We got up early every morning and did calisthenics, including multiple push-ups. Every time we did anything wrong, we had to do more pushups (I hate pushups).

- We had meals in a large chow hall, and the line moved fast. The food was excellent. In the Fort Ord dining hall I experienced my first honeydew melons and SOS (Shit on a Shingle), which is chipped creamed beef on toast. We took turns at KP (kitchen police), peeling potatoes, washing pots and pans, and cleaning the grease pit.

- We fell out for formation early every morning and marched and/or ran everywhere we went. We watched the sun come up many mornings while we were in training.

- We had inspections every day, and if your living area was not perfect, you were assigned KP or sentenced to do pushups (did I tell you I hated pushups?).

- We attended classroom training on various topics. In one class, we watched a film on venereal disease (VD), and it scared the hell out of me. I recall one scene showing a GI with swollen testicles and a penis that had turned black from VD. It left a lasting impression!

- We jumped from high towers.

- We spent a lot of time on the firing range.

- We jumped with parachutes.

- We learned hand-to-hand combat techniques.

- We swam in water in full-battle gear.

- We experienced tear gas training.

- We were in the field for ten days, simulating battle.

- We were given advanced commando training and overpracticed commando techniques.

- We performed many marching drills.

- We ran, double-stepped, or marched as a group wherever we went. We learned some rhymes to help us keep in step.

> *I had a girl in Kansas City*
> *And she had warts on her titty*
> *Sound off 1-2, once more 3-4*
> *Cadence counts 1-2-3-4; 1-2-3-4*
> *You had a good home but you left (that's right)*
> *But you don't give a damn (that's right)*
> *You work for Uncle Sam (that's right)*
> *Sound off 1-2, once more 3-4*
> *Cadence count 1-2-3-4; 1-2-3-4*

I learned all about weapons—how to take them apart, clean them, and reassemble them blindfolded. At the time, I thought it was a foolish exercise, but it proved to be invaluable in Korea where many battles were fought at night. If your weapon jammed, being able to take it apart and put it together in the dark could save your life.

I learned to fire the following weapons: a .30 caliber M-1 rifle (mainstay of the Army); the .30 caliber carbine; a small rifle; the .30 caliber BAR (Browning Automatic Rifle), which was the fastest firing automatic weapon available at the time; .30 caliber and .50 caliber machine guns; and the .45 caliber pistol. I learned how to use various types of grenades, a combat knife, and the bayonet.

During basic, I thought I would never have to use these weapons. I was wrong. In Korea, I used the M-1 rifle, the .45 caliber pistol, combat knife, hand grenades, the BAR, and the bayonet.

During training, we went through obstacle courses where live ammunition was used. It was loud and smoky. I recall being on the firing line with orders echoing in my ears: "Ready on the right, ready on the left, ready on the firing line." And then we would shoot at the target. I received sharpshooter medals for using all of these weapons.

I will never forget one demonstration of the M-1 rifle. A sergeant held up the M-1 with one hand and pointed to his groin with the other. He said, "This is my weapon (holding the rifle), and this is my gun (pointing to his groin). One is for shooting (holding the rifle), and one is for fun (pointing to his groin)."

We spent many hours in conditioning drills. Those who could not swim were given swimming lessons. I passed the swimming test so had some free time, which I spent in the PX. Our conditioning training paid great dividends in the end because I was in shape for the torturous mountain climbing I was required to do in Korea. We learned hand-to-hand combat and judo so we could kill without using a weapon. We learned how to debilitate the enemy without making a sound using a combat knife or the bayonet as a knife. I used that technique in combat. Our drill sergeant, a tough World War II veteran, had a simple approach to teaching. He demonstrated a technique and then said, "That's all there are to it."

We received weekend passes to visit the various cities around the area. I went to Salinas, California, which had a heavy Hispanic population and was known as a tough town. Even though the town had tattoo parlors, strip joints, and the normal activities that spring up near Army bases, soldiers were not welcome in many places. One sign over the door of a Salinas bar said, "No Dogs or Soldiers Allowed."

But, hell, we were young, I was a fighting liberal, and no one could deny me entrance. About five of us walked into this dingy bar, which was full of Hispanics. In broken English, the bartender said, "See the sign? It's best you leave."

We told him he would have to kick us out; we were ready for a fight and would destroy the place. He muttered something in Spanish, and quickly, we were surrounded by Mexicans. It looked like it was fight time. One of my friends said, "Get ready to shoot it out," and pulled out a .45 caliber pistol.

Suddenly, the bar went quiet.

The bartender broke the silence. "What do you want to drink?" he asked. We had a couple of beers and played some pool. Next weekend in town, the sign was down, and soldiers were welcome.

The girls were friendly in California, and I spent many happy hours in their company in Salinas, San Jose, San Francisco, and Carmel, home of the scenic seventeen-mile drive. I dated several of the rich girls from Carmel. I was always broke so I had to find cheap places to buy beer when we dated. I seldom dated the same girl more than once. The only exception was Rose, a short, thin Hispanic girl with the darkest eyes I had ever seen. She lived in Salinas and was a college student. We went to the movies and played pool; she even invited me to dinner at her house and I met her parents. Her dad was a truck driver so we got along okay. I'll always remember Rose because she saved me from getting a tattoo one crazy night. When all my other buddies were heading to the tattoo parlor, Rose persuaded me to go to the movies instead.

In California, I learned about social class. I received an education in the division between the rich and poor in our society. I saw the difference between the wealthy college girls from Carmel with their big homes and new cars and the poor Hispanic girls in Salinas. I found that some of the rich girls were nice and talked to the GIs, but others were stuck up and wanted nothing to do with the soldiers who were fighting for their freedom.

My time in San Francisco, which was 150 miles from Fort Ord, was a memorable one. A group of us went into Frisco to a bar called Finochios. Now closed, Finochios at the time was a gay bar frequented by transvestites. I wasn't the most worldly one in the bunch; remember I was a naive kid from Winona who knew of this alternative lifestyle only from reading books. But there was one guy who was even more naive than I: a Mormon kid. After a few drinks, he developed the hots for one of the girls (guys). They were all set to go to a room together when we told him to check between her (his) legs. Our Mormon friend did and had the shock of his life. We all laughed. You can bet we didn't let him forget that trip during the rest of basic training.

Another favorite city was Los Angeles, where we visited the USO center. It was a fun spot: we were served food and danced with girls to a band. Movie stars often dropped by. The one I remember was the beautiful Linda Darnell. She played in several roles opposite Tyrone Powers in the 1940s, and there she was serving soft drinks at the bar, smiling, and greeting everyone. My mother, who was an avid reader of movie star tabloids, was a huge Linda Darnell fan and was so excited when she heard that I had actually met Miss Darnell.

We often sneaked out at night and went to the beer hall on the base, which sat on a cliff with a beautiful view of the Pacific Ocean. At the beer hall, a band played nightly, and the local girls would come on the base to dance and party. Several of us

**Dances at the Soldiers Club at Fort Ord always
drew a big crowd.**

got into trouble one night when we brought a couple of girls back to the barracks to show them where we lived. The crusty old sergeant gave us extra KP for that. As I thought about it later, I realized he didn't nail us for sneaking out; he nailed us for being dumb and bringing the girls to the barracks. I imagine he was laughing at us and how many recruits did the same thing. When I returned to visit Fort Ord forty years later, I found the beer hall closed. It was in danger of falling into the ocean, which was eating away at the cliffside, and was scheduled for demolition.

When I completed basic training, there was a large ceremony. We marched in front of the general and stood at attention while the general (I do not recall his name) called our name and handed out the sharpshooter medals.

Once we received the medals, we were allowed to wear them on our class A uniforms. The class A uniform is the dress-up uniform; some of the older Army soldiers sported a chest full of medals on their class A uniform.

I received expert medals in:

- Rifle: I used the M-1 rifle with 100 percent accuracy.

- Smoke, fragmentation, incendiary, and concussion hand grenades.

- Bayonet: I learned how to fight using the bayonet.

- Carbine: I used the carbine with 90 percent accuracy.

- Pistol: I used the pistol with 90 percent accuracy.

- Auto Rifle: I used the BAR with 100 percent accuracy.

- Machine gun: I used the .30 caliber and .50 caliber machine guns with 90 percent accuracy.

My parents and my sister, Joyce, drove to California for my graduation from basic training. It was an impressive ceremony with bands playing and troops marching in review in front of the general.

I showed my parents around Fort Ord and the surrounding area. We visited Chinatown in San Francisco. After a few days, they drove back to Minnesota, and I settled into my new assignment: the Fort Ord band.

Wearing a class A uniform after completing basic training.

Here I am outside the bandroom at Fort Ord. I played the saxophone in the Fourth Division Band.

Band

After basic training, I was assigned to the Fourth Division Band at Fort Ord. I thought I had life made. I was assigned my own small private room in the barracks and was able to decorate the walls with pictures and personal items. I was issued a saxophone and clarinet and received individual lessons.

While I was at Fort Ord, we played some concerts in the area and played for basic training graduation ceremonies. I was enjoying the lifestyle of music during the day and free time at night. I was able to see a lot of the area since I had evenings and weekends free.

★ ★ ★

The North Korean Army attacked South Korea on June 25, 1950. The United States, along with the United Nations, decided to step into the fray. It was called a police action, not a war, and General Douglas MacArthur was put in charge. When I heard that the Korean War had begun, I knew my life was about to change.

That North Korean attack ended my musical career. In October 1950, the Fort Ord Band was temporarily disbanded and became infantry replacements. We were ordered to report to Camp Stoneman in San Francisco. We climbed aboard an Army bus with full-battle gear for the trip.

Camp Stoneman was a debarkation center or holding tank for troops ready to be shipped overseas. We were assigned to one-story barracks that held forty bunks, and you picked your own bunk. My only duty was to check the bulletin board daily and see if my name was there and what time to report to the bus for loading. If your name was not on the list, you were free until 8:00 a.m. the next morning, when it was time to again check the bulletin board.

I enjoyed five unassigned days at Camp Stoneman and went into San Francisco or Oakland every day. There were always several GIs that traveled together. The group changed daily because so many were being shipped out for overseas duties. Because we had no wheels, I did a lot of walking in the San Francisco area and stayed close to downtown where all the nightclubs and dance halls were located.

It was during this time that I had my X-rated experience (don't worry, Verna knows all about it). Several of us were going to San Francisco to celebrate our last days in the States. We were big tough GIs and decided to visit a whorehouse. I was one very, very nervous GI. This was my first and only experience at a whorehouse. We entered a large old mansion with chandeliers in the hallway. It was like a movie set with the madam, a lady in a long, flowing, see-through nightgown, who greeted us. She told us her policies and price. I was directed to a room.

There I was greeted by a lovely redheaded thirty-year-old woman wearing a red robe. She dropped the robe and stood in front of me totally nude. I froze. I didn't feel like a tough GI now—more like a chicken. I didn't know what to do. She told me to take off my clothes. I did. She sat on the bed and beckoned me over to her. She washed my privates and examined them. I lay on the bed with her and tried to kiss her, but she said "no kissing." Then she stroked my cock once. Poof! That was it—my great San Francisco sexual experience. When I went down to meet the guys, I told them how great it was. I still laugh at how scared I was of her.

Next morning I checked the bulletin board and found my orders to ship out. I got my full combat gear, weapons, and ammunition. It was a typical Army maneuver: hurry up and wait. I loaded on a truck and was taken to the San Francisco airport, where we boarded a Western Airline airplane.

I was on my way to Korea.

Flying soldiers in full-battle gear on a commercial airliner is not easy. Today when I fly, I often think of that trip and laugh at all the maneuvering we had to do just to find a place to put our rifles. The airline stewardess treated us well, serving us liquor and beer. She knew we were headed for combat and was showing her respect for our service to our country.

Before being shipped overseas, I went to a library and looked up where Korea was. At that time, I knew nothing about that tiny country south of China.

I was excited and afraid. I was nineteen years old, traveling to a new land and beginning an adventure.

An adventure where I would be fighting for my life.

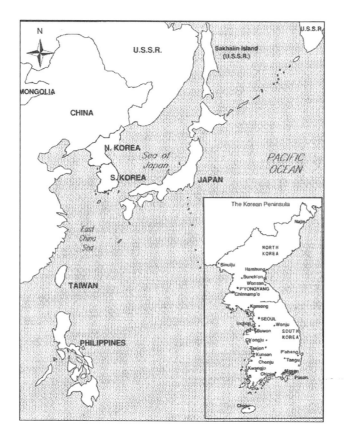

CHAPTER THREE

HONOLULU AND WAKE STOPOVERS ON THE WAY TO KOREA

I loaded on an airplane in San Francisco and flew to Hawaii. I was thrilled; this was my first airplane flight. Peering out the window, I studied the vast expanse of the Pacific Ocean and wondered what was in store for me.

When the airplane landed in Honolulu, we were given a six-hour layover, but it turned into an overnight, a unique opportunity courtesy of an enterprising mechanic. One GI bragged he could sabotage the plane and arrange for us to have an overnight in Hawaii—if we paid him. We took up a collection, and lo and behold, the plane had motor trouble in Honolulu. We could not take off until morning, which meant we got to spend a night on the beach in Honolulu. I still do not know how he did it. My guess is he had prior information that there was engine trouble and used the information to collect some money.

I was awestruck by the beauty of Hawaii. It is hard to explain how impressed I was with the warmth and beaches on this island. It was a drastic change from Winona. The sand glistened in the sun on the massive beach, which was lined with huge luxurious hotels. There were girls all over the beach, friendly girls. Since we were in battle gear, we took turns guarding the equipment as we stripped down to shorts to take a quick dip in the ocean. It was a funny sight to see all these young soldiers chasing around on the beach in khaki shorts.

When evening came, we went to a huge hotel, stored our equipment in the lobby, and drew straws to guard the equipment. There must have been more than fifty young GIs in battle gear roaming around that luxurious hotel—what a sight.

I ordered a beer at the hotel bar and was shocked to find it was a $1.00. (I was from Winona, the home of the ten-cent beer.)

I walked around the city and could not get enough of the atmosphere of Hawaii. Alas, morning came, and we had to board the airplane for Japan via Wake Island.

Wake Island: Revisiting World War II History

We had a short layover on Wake Island. Wake is a small island with only twelve miles of coastline. It had a well-equipped Army base with a huge airport. We ate a meal in the dining hall, spent some time cleaning and checking our weapons, and were given a tour of the island.

We flew to Hawaii, Wake Island, and then Japan in this type of airplane.

I couldn't believe how small the island was and how much battle history was packed into it. Here was where our troops held off the Japanese in World War II. Rusted tanks and artillery guns, still lying by the roadside, served as a reminder of the ferocious battle for Wake Island. It took place in December 1941 when the Japanese attacked the island and the US forces held for twelve days before surrendering. A total of 108 Americans and 880 Japanese died in the battle. The US prisoners were taken to POW camps. Six Americans were beheaded in one of the most heinous acts of the Japanese Army, according to our Army tour guide. I was in awe that this small place could hold so much history and the memories of so many who had died here. In this place, scarred by conflict, I wondered, "What is war all about?"

I was about to find out. I had no idea what was in store for me. On that day, I was more tourist than soldier, still excited about my first airplane ride and first trip across the ocean.

Wake Island

We landed at Wake Airport then
toured the island. Wake Island was
a small pocket of land loaded with
battle history and reminders of World
War II: bunkers (top) and pillboxes
(bottom right).

CHAPTER FOUR

CAMP DRAKE IN JAPAN

From Wake Island, we flew to Tokyo, Japan. We were loaded on buses and taken to Camp Drake, a large training camp in the mountains, twenty miles from Tokyo. When I reported there, I received my assignment to Third Squad, Third Platoon, Baker Company, Fifteenth Regiment, Third Division. I reported to the company commander and met my squad members and Sergeant Dick McKay, my squad leader who was later killed in action. They had been training for several weeks and made me feel welcome.

The army was establishing a program of inculcating ROK (Republic of Korea) soldiers into American squads. Each squad of seven men had three or four ROKs with them. They were not the best fighters, but they could fire an M-1 rifle and gave us additional firepower. In combat, we had an understanding with them: If they ran from combat, we would shoot them in the back. "Stay and live; run and die" was our motto. I had great respect for these soldiers, and none that I knew tried to run from battle.

The Third Division patch (top) went on my left arm. Fifteenth Regimental crest was positioned on my shoulder.

At Camp Drake, we received refresher infantry training in self-defense techniques and spent a lot of time on the rifle range. We attended interesting classes on Korean culture and military tactics.

We were in Japan for a couple of weeks, and while there, I had liberty. I toured Tokyo in a rickshaw, paying for the ride with black-market cigarettes. GIs received free cigarette rations. The military used US-printed script notes instead of money in Japan. I shopped at small vendors and sent pictures and trinkets home.

I still recall the hustle, bustle, and crowded conditions of Tokyo's narrow streets. The Japanese all bowed when we were with them. Many of the women were dressed in traditional attire. I drank Japanese beer (which was okay) in the small Japanese taverns that barely seated twenty people. When we went to town, we always traveled in groups of three or four and carried our .45 pistols on our hips.

Many places in Tokyo were off-limits to American soldiers, but one place we were allowed to patronize were the Japanese bathhouses. On my trip to a bathhouse, I was greeted by women dressed in formal kimono attire. Before you could enter the hot tubs in the bathhouse, you had to be clean, and it was the job of the women in the kimonos to bathe you. First, they took off their kimonos, working only in white bras and panties. Then they removed my clothes and gave me a hand-scrubbing bath. Only after this procedure was I allowed to enter the large tubs, where I sat in warm water up to my neck. It was a fun experience.

Japan was a short reprieve. All too soon we had orders to load up and prepare for a beach landing in North Korea. I was apprehensive.

I was headed for combat.

CHAPTER FIVE

FIRST DAY IN KOREA: THE WONSAN LANDING

On a cold November morning in 1950, we loaded trucks and traveled forty miles to a large harbor in Yokohama, port of Moji, Japan. My eyes got big when I saw all the naval ships in the harbor. I boarded a former Japanese troop carrier, the *USS General Killian Waigal,* which had been commissioned by the US Navy. I was carrying full-battle gear. I had my knapsack, M-1 rifle, ammunition, grenades, sleeping bag, mess kit, etc.

As we sailed up the east coast of North Korea, I stood on deck and watched this large armada of ships sailing toward North Korea. It was like a scene from a movie—large battleships and aircraft carriers bouncing on the waves. This was my first experience on a large, crowded ship in rough seas. The ceilings were low so when you walked around you had to keep your head down. I was assigned a bunk in the lower level. The bunks, designed for the Japanese, were small; my feet hung over the edge. We were at sea for several days (and, of course, I was a little seasick).

We arrived at Wonsan, North Korea, and the ship dropped anchor. I waited for my orders to assemble on deck in full-battle gear. Charlie Edmond, one of my buddies, said, "I can see the bleak, cold outline of the North Korean coast through the streaked porthole of the ship." Charlie was a chubby-faced kid who had been studying philosophy and poetry in college before joining the Army. We spent hours discussing philosophy and religion. He even talked me into enrolling into a correspondence psychology course while I was in Korea. I carried my textbook in my pack. When I was wounded, that textbook was left behind in Korea, tucked into the bottom of my sleeping bag. Charlie, my philosopher friend, ended up staying in the Army and flew helicopters in Vietnam.

The Sea of Japan was rough on the day of our landing, and it was cold. The *Missouri, Wisconsin,* and *St. Paul*—three large battleships— as well as cruisers pounded the

This was my first view of North Korea. Little did I know I would end up in the mountains in the background. They looked so tall and frightening.

beach and mountains with a hell of a lot of firepower. You could watch the airplanes and hear the bombs as they exploded.

On November 11, 1950 (Veteran's Day), a windy day with below-freezing temperatures, I made my first beach landing. I nervously crawled down a swinging wet rope ladder (no training) while the ship was rocking and rolling or, as they say in the Navy, pitching a lot. It was very difficult, and I kind of fell into the landing craft. I felt incredibly awkward trying to stand up in the rocking landing boat with all

While waiting to crawl down the rope ladder to load the landing craft, a minesweeper hit a mine, and there was a large explosion. It was the first of many explosions I heard in Korea.

This hole (bottom right) is the result of a sixteen-inch gun from the battleships. They caused massive damage, and when we landed, I saw for the first time the total destruction that war brings to an area.

my equipment. I boarded the landing ship, an LST number #883, at 1600 (4:00 p.m.) and landed on the beach at Wonsan at 2100 (9:00 p.m.) after five hours of bouncing on the ocean.

By the time the landing craft hit the beach, I had chills and was sweating at the same time. This was my introduction to Korea: I'd been stuffed in a Japanese troop ship, crawled down a wet slippery movable rope ladder, been bounced up and down in rough seas until I was seasick and throwing up, and then dropped on a rocky beach.

The battleships continued pounding the shoreline with heavy fire, and the airplanes kept flying overhead, laying down fire to protect us. The guy next to me, a veteran of World War II and a former prisoner of war, suddenly went crazy. He shot himself in the foot and yelled, "I can't take it again." Why was he panicking? I wondered. He was experienced; he knew about war. I was a green kid who didn't know what I had gotten into.

DONALD R. SONSALLA

Landing at Wonsan

Fifteenth Regiment pictures of November 1950 landing at Wonsan.

I heard enemy small arms fire. Bullets whizzed over my head and ricocheted off the landing craft. I saw Bernie Stover, a skinny, seventeen-year-old kid who enlisted to show his girlfriend that he was brave, go limp in front of me, blood gushing from his head. In an instant, he was gone, taking a .50 caliber through his helmet. I was scared. For the first time, I smelled blood spilled in battle, Bernie's blood, and I can still smell it in my mind today and experience the chill of fear. Bernie was the first member of our company killed during the landing. I witnessed my first death in combat but not my last. It was weird; I don't recall having any feelings in that moment when Bernie left this world. I simply plowed ahead; I had to complete the landing and reach cover. I jumped out of the landing craft into cold water up to my waist and sloshed through the water and ran up on the beach.

Maybe that is when I truly became a soldier, when I learned to turn off my emotions and carry on. It was a different world. It was like a surrealistic dream, so unreal and so full of horror and fear.

I was on shore, and suddenly, the enemy stopped shooting. They disappeared into the mountains. The only noise was the shelling from the battleships and airplanes flying over. I could hear the explosions in the mountains. We were ordered to load up on Army and Marine deuce-and-a-half trucks (2½ ton) and move into the mountains. I stared up at the mountains and could not believe how tall and menacing they were. The truck I was assigned to would not start, so I had to stay on the beach while the others moved on. Finally, hours later, we got the truck started, loaded up, and drove into the mountains on a narrow, winding road. We caught up to the rest of the company and found disaster.

They had been ambushed and suffered heavy casualties. It sickened me to see the dead soldiers lying on the roadside, the damage to the vehicles, and the wounded men, who were being treated on an emergency basis while waiting to be transferred to a MASH unit. I was lucky that our truck had broken down. Otherwise, I would have been in that ambush.

Ambushes were routine in Korea. I witnessed the deaths of many GIs (see body above) and the destruction of a lot of equipment.

CHAPTER SIX

A MOUNTAIN VACATION
AT MAJON-NI

Military Importance

After we made the beach landing in November, our company moved up the mountains to replace the First Marine Regiment at Majon-ni, a village and mountain base thirty miles west of Wonsan. It was estimated that the enemy strength was around fifteen thousand within a radius of fifteen miles of Majon-ni. The First Battalion (that was me) was assigned to relieve the Third Battalion of the First Marines, and the Third Battalion was to relieve the Second Battalion of the First Marine Regiment at a place called Half-Way Point on the Wonsan-Majon-ni route.

One of our jobs was to keep the road open.

A system of truck convoys was established. They drove to Majon-ni one day and returned the next day with the wounded. Seriously wounded personnel were evacuated by air. All convoys were escorted by armed units to deter an ambush.

My first trip to Majon-ni was harrowing. Piled into the back of an Army truck, we tackled the thirty miles up crooked, winding, narrow mountain roads. Several tanks led the way. It was a scary ride. The road was right on the edge of a cliff.

Artillery shells had made holes in the road. Looking over the edge, I peered straight down hundreds of feet and got an eerie feeling of falling over the edge. Eventually, I got used to mountain transportation. After trudging in the mountains for a couple of days, I lost all fear of falling off the edge.

Majon-ni was an important transportation hub in a mountain pass, and by establishing a base there, you controlled all the rural roads in the area. There was major enemy activity, including considerable guerilla action and a strong contingent of regular North Korean Army trying to control the area. The Fifteenth Regimental Combat Team's mission was to eliminate the guerrillas and North Korean Army and secure the Wonsan-Majon-ni-Tongyang road and a ninety-mile stretch of

Top: The whole time I was in Korea I was in awe of the massive mountains. They were an enemy and a friend. This was my home on Majon-ni.

Left: This is a typical ridge in Korea. At Majon-ni, we established our post on top of a ridge and had control of the area. To give you some perspective of the size of the mountains, look closely; you can see the GIs. Most of the trees had been destroyed by artillery and mortar fire.

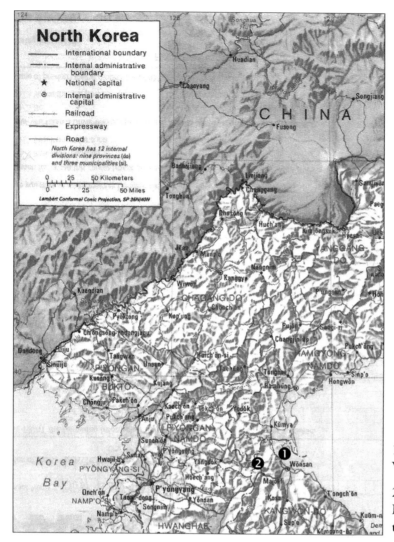

1. Landed here in Wonsan.

2. Then headed to Majon-ni high in the mountains.

the area. If you controlled the high mountains, you controlled the roads. Official documents show that there were nightly attacks along this mountain road.

The mountains were the size of the US Rockies in the two-thousand- to eight-thousand-foot range. We established our company base on a ridge more than three thousand feet high with a clear view of the valley. There were a lot of cliffs and frighteningly steep slopes. I remember writing home about the majesty of the mountains and the beauty of the surroundings. I soon forgot about the beauty and only saw the obstacles it presented.

Typical mountain roads in North Korea.

Majon-ni, The Village

Majon-ni sounds like an exotic name, but in reality, it was a small rural village, thirty miles in a mountain valley west of Wonsan, North Korea. This was high mountainous country with many small villages. Most of the huts in the villages had a heating system made of clay and hard mud. They were hollow under the floor, and on one end of the house, they had a fireplace. This was the Korean family's stove, and they always had a bowl cooking on the stove (fireplace). The chimney ran the length and under the floor (thus heating the building). Windows were of rice paper.

The villages were largely self-sufficient. They raised their own food, gathered their own fuel, and made their own clothing. They had no modern transportation and little contact with the outside world. They were a rural people with no schooling and little knowledge of modern conveniences.

A common sight in Korea was a *papa-san* (name for a Korean man) carrying two buckets on a yoke on his shoulders to the fields. These buckets, called honey buckets, contained human waste. We called them shit repositories. Korean families kept the buckets in the house, used them as toilets, and then carried them to the field. They had a strong pungent smell.

War was hard on these small villages. We often destroyed them, burning their huts, the people's

When I was in Korea, I bought this picture of a man carrying honey buckets. It is hung in my bathroom. When I meditate in the bathroom, I have thoughts of freezing bathroom experiences in Korea.

A typical North Korean family and their living quarters.

homes. This turned them into refugees, and it was not uncommon to return from patrol with refugees as well as prisoners.

Foxhole Living

You get the best view of war—its horror and death—from a foxhole.

Our company was housed in foxholes on top of a mountain. A foxhole is simply a hole dug in the ground. It was hard to dig a hole because the mountains were mostly rock and the ground was frozen and covered with snow. Sometimes we fired weapons into the soil to loosen it, which enabled us to dig the foxholes faster. Records indicate that the frost line at that time in North Korea was down eighteen inches. I made myself as comfortable as possible in my assigned foxhole.

If there was time, you reinforced the foxhole with sandbags. I also reinforced my foxhole with logs cut from pine trees. I placed logs and branches on top to give me protection from the elements and from incoming fire. The nearest foxhole to me was about ten feet away, so we could have a constant chatter going on when we were not under fire or maintaining quiet at night listening for the enemy.

One of my foxhole buddies, Ramon, shared his experience digging his first foxhole, "It was dark, and I pulled a frozen log in front of my foxhole. In the morning, I looked and discovered it was the body of a frozen enemy soldier."

Ramon, a Filipino, had been a guerrilla fighter in his homeland. He started fighting the Japanese in his teens. Barely five feet tall, he was adept at using a knife, which he clutched in his teeth as he jumped into foxholes to slay the enemy. He had joined the US Army in hopes of becoming a US citizen someday, and he did become one.

Usually, there were two soldiers in a foxhole. Thus, one was always on guard duty. I had three foxhole buddies in November and December, all of whom were either wounded or killed. My foxhole buddies' job

Often a foxhole was my home in Korea. Sometimes I shared it with my foxhole buddy.

was to cover me when I was being used as a sniper.

At night, in a foxhole, pulling guard duty and not under attack, you can have a lot of philosophical thoughts. It was a time for day-dreaming or planning for the future, for a time when I would leave Korea. I never doubted that I would not get out alive. I had witnessed many of my foxhole buddies getting killed, but for some reason, I felt I would make it through the war. It always paid to have positive thoughts.

Land Mines

I learned to place land mines in front of our position and map the route for safe passage. There were two types of mines. One you sim-ply planted in the ground; actually, all we did was cover it with snow. The other, more power-ful type, which could knock out a tank, had to be buried in the ground. You attached a thin

When I returned to Korea in 1985, I visited Hill 337, and the foxholes were still there. Here is a picture of a sandbag-reinforced foxhole.

trip wire and hooked the wire to a tree or something about ten feet away. The mines were nicknamed Bouncing Betty and Bouncing Betsy because if they were triggered they would bounce up about three feet and explode spreading shrapnel all over. They were lethal weapons—to our enemies and, sometimes, to us.

One sad day in November, a replacement soldier from Stillwater, Minnesota, stepped in front of our position to look over the mountain scenery, walked too far in front of the foxholes, and stepped on a Bouncing Betty. He was killed on the spot. We had warned him to study the mine map and not go too far out in front. It was his first day on tour. Bob Grodhaus, a beer-drinking redneck from Ohio and a very tough soldier, told me that was "the hardest death for him to witness"—it occurred just after Bob learned that his brother had been killed in action.

Defending Our Position

I was in an all-night firefight on my first night after arriving at Majon-ni. I was doing night watch in my foxhole when we were hit. The enemy came in waves. The North Korean Army was testing us, the new outfit on the hill. The enemy got close enough

42

to throw grenades. One grenade wounded Andy, my foxhole buddy, in the arms. I experienced the shock waves of the grenade, but he caught the shrapnel. Flares were shot up in the air by our artillery, and when they exploded, a parachute would open up and the flares would float down giving us some light.

Things happened so fast my head was swimming. I became a robot and acted without emotion. I fired and fired. They attacked us all night, from 0200 (2:00 a.m.) to 05:45 (5:45 a.m.). We could not go out in front and get a body count because our artillery continued to lay a barrage of fire in front of us.

That night I got my first kill.

It was a North Korean soldier, who was close enough to me to throw a grenade. As he was moving his arm back to throw, I shot him and watched his head explode. I can still see the face of that soldier lifting his arm to throw the grenade and my bullets tearing him apart. One second, he had a face, and the next, he was nothing but blood and a falling body. This feeling of killing can never be erased. It is embedded, actually burned, into my brain forever. I became a killer on that day.

I still flashback to that moment. Sometimes, when I am watching a baseball game on television and I see the pitcher rear back to throw, I see that soldier, grenade in hand, and I watch him die, again.

I continued shooting and saw bodies fall, but all of us were shooting and throwing hand grenades so who hit what I don't really know. I only knew that it was dark except for the flares, that I was scared, and that this was war.

This poem, written by an unknown author, describes my reaction to this first day of combat.

> The infantryman who has survived
> His first combat experience and
> Who returns to the safety and
> Camaraderie of his buddies, soon
> Realizes that he has experienced
> A major exploration of his soul
> Something that most other men
> Will never understand

Next day it was quiet, except for hearing artillery or small arms fire in the distance. Suddenly, I heard airplanes and saw a large number of Marine Corsairs, US Air Force Sabre Jets, and Australian P-51s flying over, strafing, and dropping napalm as well as other bombs on enemy positions in the mountains. This was the only time I saw the Air Force, Marines, and Australians flying cover together on the same mission. The enemy gave no return fire. Because of our control of the skies, the enemy was forced to move at night.

While we were in the mountains, we were shelled almost every night with artillery. You could hear the shells whistling over your head. You could tell by the sound how close they were to you and also you could tell if they were outgoing (our forces) or incoming (the enemy). Almost every night the enemy would charge up the mountain trying to dislodge us. Each day we had to place more land mines and check the bodies of the enemy, looking for plans, identification, and souvenirs. The fighting was intense, and each night I had several kills. There was almost an endless stream of the enemy coming up every night to be slaughtered. Our company paid a toll as well, and I lost several foxhole buddies. It seemed I would just learn their names and where they were from, and then they were either wounded or killed. While I was in combat, I was promoted to private first class.

The night of November 16, 1950, we heard bugles. They signaled the beginning of a three-day fight. The enemy kept charging up the hills, and we kept holding them off. It is hard to explain how many and how fast they came. It was like a crowd rushing out after a football game at a stadium. The land mines took a terrible toll on the enemy, but the enemy soldiers just stepped over the broken bodies of their comrades. They charged and got so close to my position that I could see their facial expressions as I pulled the trigger.

I shot and shot. They fell right in front of me. I shot an enemy soldier who had reached the foxhole next to me, and one of his legs below the knee exploded. He was treated by our medics and sent back as a POW.

We held our position, and in front of our foxholes, bodies were stacked like cordwood. I recall sitting in my foxhole and talking about how it was like a bowling game—they would line up and we would shoot and they would fall down.

The battle ended, and I was exhausted. I felt relief from the killing. The company commander informed us that more than four hundred North Korean soldiers had been killed or wounded. After the fight, we searched the bodies of the enemy. At first, it was weird walking amid all those dead bodies, but it became commonplace. In Korea, you quickly lost your fear of dead bodies. After the battle was over, it was time to drink a beer (we had beer rations), sit back, and play cards.

To ease the pain of killing others, we laughed a lot and refused to think about our losses. We drank and became quite inventive in our quest for alcohol. We would take our beer can ration, open it up, and let it freeze. After it was frozen, we would pour out the alcohol, mix it with snow, and have a snowball drink. After that, we would melt the sludge in the can and have near beer.

What is that old saying? There's no rest for the wicked. We must have been wicked because the North Korean Army hit us again. We captured several of the enemy and were surprised to find some Chinese troops among them.

Official reports showed that on November 22, a patrol was in the same area and again the enemy had assembled. Another twenty-two enemy soldiers were killed in the firefight.

On November 23, there was another night attack; two enemy were killed and the rest taken as prisoners.

Because of the nightly attacks, a heavy mortar company was attached to the First Battalion. We were receiving heavy casualties, and the wounded were evacuated daily.

The Joys of a Patrol

Besides holding our position, we constantly patrolled. The majority of our patrol action was with either a squad of six soldiers or one- or two-man patrols. The purpose was to go behind enemy lines, establish a position, and help in the calling in of air strikes and air support. The First Marine Air Wing gave us close support.

One night a squad was sent out to patrol and did not come back. John Pitts, one of our squad members, was on that patrol. Bobby McCoun and I went out in front of the line (we had to be careful of land mines) to do a fast search for the missing patrol. We found John and two other dead US soldiers at the bottom of the mountain tied to a tree. They had their hands tied behind their back and had been stabbed over and over, probably with a bayonet. It looked as if the enemy had tried to burn them (probably in retaliation for our napalm bombing). We were getting ready to cut them down when a company of enemy soldiers supported by a tank came up the road and started shooting at us. We fired back and retreated quickly back up the

hill to our line. The bullets were whizzing over our heads, and the soldier who was aiming the tank's cannon must have been off target that day since the exploding shells were over fifty yards away. A Marine Corsair flew down and strafed the enemy troops, helping us get away to our line.

Later, a different squad went back, but the bodies were gone. It was common in combat to take the GI bodies away just to bug us. John Pitts was listed as missing in action on November 21, 1950.

This poem describes the strong feeling I have for those missing in action:

Missing In Action

It is one thing to die for your country. It has an ending.
It is another to just disappear from the face of the earth
Leaving no trace of a life that held so much promise.
To be forgotten as if his life did not matter. This is not right.

Years later, in 1996, during the Korean War Memorial dedication in Washington, DC, a man approached the men carrying the Baker Company Third Division sign and asked if we knew about his brother, John Pitts, who had been listed as MIA. We told him that he had been killed and how we saw the body. He cried on the spot, hugged us, and said he felt better knowing what had happened.

After viewing some of our soldiers who had been captured, bound, and killed—I swore that I would never be taken prisoner.

After the three-day fight, I went out on a six-man patrol to meet up with the Third Battalion, but we encountered heavy resistance and had to dig in for the night. A second squad patrol was sent out to support us. Eventually, the entire Baker and Charlie Company force joined us. After an all-day firefight, we were victorious, killing more than one hundred enemy soldiers and capturing a hundred more.

One day half of our company hiked down the mountain about ten miles to Kunu-ri, a small village. Our mission was to rout the enemy housed in the village. We attacked the village, and the enemy retaliated with small arms and machine guns but no mortar fire. We thought this was unusual, since we later found twenty-five unused mortars in the huts. We fought for over two hours until they surrendered. We captured over two hundred prisoners, more than the number in our company; we counted twenty-five killed and fifty wounded. In our company, eight guys were wounded and evacuated to Wonsan. There were about one hundred refugees who asked for protection and came back with us to be taken to Wonsan. It was quite a sight to see—us walking back to base with a sea of refugees and prisoners carrying their wounded. The prisoners were put on trucks and taken back to Wonsan to be interrogated. We had good information about enemy troop movements since we had South Korean soldiers in our outfit who could speak their language. Sadly, we burned all the buildings in the village and happily destroyed a lot of weapons that the enemy had stored. There was a series of explosions as the ammunition and grenades kept exploding in the buildings that we had set on fire.

Another company mission was to clear out the village of Kumden-ni. When we entered the village, we had little resistance. The enemy had fled and left a lot of weapons in the huts. Again, we destroyed the weapons and the huts. What a waste. And again we took the refugees back to our base. Refugees were trucked to Wonsan, where they were given the option to go to South Korea or to stay in the area in refugee camps. From what I learned, most went to South Korea.

I was sent on a three-man patrol the next day and was walking through a village when I spotted five enemy tanks along with soldiers coming down the road. There we were: three guys with two M-1 rifles and my BAR facing a tank. Talk about a helpless feeling. We left fast before they saw us, skedaddled back to base, and reported the sighting. The enemy was getting ready for a counterattack. We spread out more land mines in front of us. Several US Third Division tanks were moving up to give us support from the rear.

One other day, I was in a squad that moved into the valley below us and found ammunition dumps in several straw-thatched shacks. We radioed for artillery fire, and the Air Force came in on a bombing run. I watched planes swoop in firing rockets, leaving a trail of smoke, and boom, one hell of an explosion. Two days later, a company of North Koreans charged up the hill. We repulsed the attack and killed 134 enemy soldiers. Three soldiers from our company were killed and three wounded.

While on one patrol, I found telephone wires leading from our outpost to a couple of huts in a small village. Our mission was to severely punish those who were wiretapping. Our squad burned down the huts with the telephones in them.

Destroying a Temple

In war, we destroy so much—lives, homes, roads, the land. Some destruction stays with us forever, and this was the case with the Buddhist temple.

I was leading a squad of five men while on patrol in the mountains of North Korea. I was way out in front and came upon a small Buddhist temple near the top of the mountain. It was about thirty feet by thirty feet and made of rice paper and small branches. It had a lot of bells and paper lanterns hanging by the door. It reminded me of the beauty of St. Stanislaus Church in Winona and, being curious, I wanted to explore the beauty of this temple.

I slid open the door and marveled at all the small statues lining the walls and the many banners hanging from the ceiling.

In the middle of the room was a Buddhist statue, about four feet tall, surrounded by smaller statues.

Suddenly, a North Korean soldier jumped out from behind the large Buddha statue and took a shot at me with his rifle. Luckily he missed. I unloaded my BAR at him with all twenty rounds. I shattered the Buddha statue into a thousand pieces and hit the soldier in the head. He fell down in a pool of blood. I loaded in another clip and emptied that clip into him.

Words are hard to explain the emotions I was going through when I was shooting the Gook that took aim at me in the temple. I was possessed and full of rage and kept emptying clip after clip into the lifeless, bloody corpse. I had severed the head from the body and kept shooting at the head. Then I kicked the head and sent it sailing across the room. Enraged, I reloaded and shot up all the statues. "Who shoots at people in a church?" I cried.

Finally, Bobby, a fellow squad member, walked up to me and grabbed me by the shoulder. He said, "He's dead; let's go." I kicked the head again as I left.

Standing outside, I threw in a fragmentary and an incendiary grenade and burned the temple to the ground. I then turned to the squad and said, "Let's get out of here. The smoke will bring the Chinks."

It was a heinous act for which I have paid many times. When walking and I see a stone, I will kick the stone and my mind plays a game with me. I am back in that temple again, seeing the lifeless, bloody head that I had just kicked.

War is hell, and the memories are worse.

A typical Buddhist temple.

An enemy soldier was hidden behind a large
Buddha like this one and took a shot at me.

Fifty years later, I visited Korea, and at the foot of the hill where I was wounded was a Buddhist temple. I entered the temple and met a Buddhist monk. Through an interpreter, I explained how I had burned and destroyed the temple in North Korea and carried that guilt with me for many years. The Buddhist monk and I shared some Korean tea. He blessed me and gave me a statue of Buddha for forgiveness. It was an act of cleansing.

I kept that Buddha statue in a place of honor, and later I gave my Buddha statue as a good luck charm to my granddaughter, Dana, when she received her commission in the Army. She

Picture of my granddaughter Dana's combat boots and the Buddha that was given to me.

went on to the University of Tennessee Law School, passed the bar, and is now a JAG officer. I hope the Buddha continues to bring Captain Dana Neumann good luck. In 2011, she was stationed at Camp Yongson in Seoul, South Korea, an area where I did considerable urban fighting in March 1951.

A Guy and His BAR

The Browning Automatic Rifle (BAR) was an integral part of me in Korea. I have great respect and admiration for this weapon. Modern weapons have replaced it, but it holds a special spot in my heart, since it saved my life many times.

Today a BAR is hanging on the wall in my home, and I look at it now and then. The BAR is air cooled, gas operated, and magazine fed. A shoulder type weapon, it provides selective fire as a semi- or full-automatic weapon. It has a 20-round magazine, weighs 18.5 pounds, and is 47 inches long. It can fire 550 rounds per minute. It has an effective range of 600 yards (one-third of a mile). It fires a standard .30 caliber rifle cartridge.

During the Korean War, the BAR was used as an essential weapon in an American rifle squad and was used by snipers.

I wrote this poem several years ago, and in a small way, it explains how I feel about my BAR.

My BAR
By Don Sonsalla

Do you wonder why that BAR
Is hanging on the wall in my den?
You know, I rarely take it down
But I touch and caress it now and then

It's rather slow and heavy
By standards of today
But not too many years ago
It swept the enemy away.

It held its own in battles
Through snow and cold away so far
And I had one just like it
My treasured dear old BAR

It went ashore with me
In nineteen fifty you see
It stormed the beach at Wonsan
Through a bullet-riddled sea.

The enemy knew its strident bark,
The North Koreans its deadly sting
The rocky caves of Korea
Resounded with its deadly ring.

It climbed a hill or two
With men who wouldn't stop.
And left the nation's banner
Flying high on the very top.

It poked its nose in Seoul,
Screamed an angry roar
And it took the Third Division
From the frozen Chosin Reservoir

Well, time moves on and things improve
With rifles and with men
And that is why the two of us
Are sitting in my den.

Picture of a GI shooting with a BAR.

Being a Sniper

I qualified as a sharpshooter in basic training and was familiar with various weapons. Without a scope and with a tripod, the BAR was a superior sniper's rifle. My first experience serving as a sniper in November was to crawl onto a high, unprotected ridge with binoculars, assisted by an ammo carrier, an ROK soldier, and a radio man. I observed the enemy soldiers about six hundred yards (six football fields) away moving down into a valley. I zeroed in on the leader and shot him in his middle area. I saw him fall. As soon as I shot, all hell broke loose, and a lot of small arms fire and mortar fire started landing in our direction. I got out of there fast and ran through the minefields to the safety of our perimeter. After I was safely back in my foxhole, I meditated about the power I had to take life. I decided to stop waxing philosophical thoughts and think only, "It was him or me."

The next time I was sent out as a sniper, I was located in a crevice behind a huge rock on the mountainside. I had K-rations, an ammo carrier, and a radioman. I took down three of the enemy ammunition bearers who were moving from one small hut to another in the village. While I was in position just above the village, I saw Marine Corsairs flying below me dropping napalm bombs on the enemy. We were close enough that I could feel the heat, even though the temperature was below zero. When the planes started their strafing run over your head and the shell casings fell on you, they were hot and you could get burned from the empty casings. I laughed to myself and told my ammo carrier, "It was about time the Marines did something for us." The Marine pilots were awesome, and many times, they banked their planes at low level and gave us thumbs up.

I continued to serve as a sniper in November and December. My total kill of thirteen was recorded by putting notches on my BAR handle. Later in February and March, I again was assigned as a sniper and notched twelve more. I acquired twenty-five nightmares that haunt me nightly during my time as a sniper. I can recall each shot.

Friendly Fire

If ever there were a stupid euphemism or oxymoron, friendly fire is it. Friendly fire is the firing of weapons at your own troops by mistake. I hated the term "friendly fire." There is nothing friendly about being shot, bombed, or showered with rockets, no matter whose hand is on the trigger or the fire button.

Friendly fire happened to me while I was in Korea. We had several enemy troops moving up the mountain in front of our position. The temperature was below zero, snow had fallen, and the ground was covered with several inches of snow. We laid out a large red banner on the ground indicating our position to the pilot. An Air Force Shooting Star jet came zooming over our position. The jet stayed high in the air and started to make a strafing run shooting up the area. But, a big but, by mistake, he strafed our position. He was strafing behind the red banner rather than in front of it. He only made one run over our position, but it made us scramble. We were yelling, cussing, and keeping our heads under cover. So this is what sitting ducks felt like. The SOB was in a warm plane while we were freezing our asses off and he is shooting at us. We were one unhappy group. I had been scared in combat before, but this was a different feeling—because there was nothing I could do to stop this air jockey from shooting at us. I understood at that point, how the enemy felt when our planes were raising hell with them. Luckily, the jets stayed up high and no damage was done, except to our pride.

Gourmet Dining in Korea; Thanksgiving 1950

General MacArthur promised the troops that we would be sitting down to Thanksgiving dinner. Thanksgiving came, and there was a lull in the fighting. Turkey was brought to the front line and cooked over camp stoves. By the time the hot turkey hit the plate, it was frozen. However, it was the first time we had something other than C-rations.

While I was in Korea, almost all of my meals were C-rations and K-rations. C-rations came in cans, and we had to open the can and decide whether to eat it hot or cold. K-rations were dried rations.

In a C-rations pack, there were cans of beef steak, ham and eggs chopped, ham slices, turkey loaf, beans and wieners, spaghetti and meatballs, ham and lima beans, meatballs and beans, boned chicken, chicken and noodles, and spiced beef.

Fruit cans offered applesauce, fruit cocktail, peaches, pears, and various jams.

Others items in our rations were crackers, peanut butter, cheese, chocolate, pecan roll, fruit cake, pound cake, cookies, cocoa, white bread, and cigarettes. Needless to say, there was a lot of trading to meet our individual tastes.

I was impressed with the C-rations, and we had an enjoyable time preparing meals from the cans. One of my favorites was taking cocoa powder and mixing it with snow to create a great dessert. Beans and franks were my all-time favorite entrée.

Frank Romero, a good medic and one of my foxhole friends, had Tabasco sauce sent to him, and he put it on everything. We teased him a lot about his taste for spicy food. He was Hispanic with a heavy accent and came from the 187th Airborne looking for action. He hailed from California and hated the cold weather.

We received cans of Sterno, which when lit served as an efficient little stove.

Cooking presented a problem. Sometime we had the luxury of a large fire; other times we had to make an individual stove from a cut can like this.

Soldier Essentials

An important item for every soldier was our dog tags. Each soldier wore a metal dog tag around his neck on a chain. It contained his name, serial number, and blood type. My blood type is A, and this was helpful information when I was wounded and needed a live blood transfusion.

One of the Army's amazing inventions was the small can opener we carried with our dog tags. It didn't look like much, but it really worked.

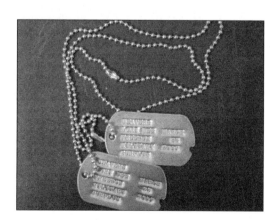 

Left: Dogtags. Top: Our handy can openers were called P-38s.

Ambush Alley

While we were housed in the mountains, all of our supplies were brought in from Wonsan via trucks through narrow mountain valley roads. The enemy had been harassing the transportation route in the area for several days. A contingent of over three hundred North Korean guerillas and regular Army had blockaded a section of the highway called Ambush Alley. The blockade, made of heavy logs, had trapped several companies of South Korean Marines that were housed just north of us.

On November 21, 1950, our company received orders called "Operation Revenge" to eliminate the enemy in that section.

Prior to entering Ambush Alley, I thought of one of my favorite poems in high school, Lord Alfred Tennyson's "The Charge of the Light Brigade":

> *Cannon to the right of them,*
> *Cannon to the left of them,*
> *Cannon in front of them*
> > *Volley'd and thunder'd;*
> *Storm'd at with shot and shell,*
> *Boldly they rode and well,*
> *Into the jaws of Death,*
> *Into the mouth of Hell*
> > *Rode the six hundred.*

> *"Forward, the Light Brigade!"*
> *Was there a man dismay'd?*
> *Not tho' the soldier new*
> > *Someone had blunder'd:*
> *Theirs not to make reply,*
> *Theirs not to reason why,*
> *Theirs but to do and die:*
> *Into the valley of Death*
> > *Rode the six hundred.*

In Operation Revenge, half of our company, including my squad, walked down to the bottom of the mountain and loaded on trucks ready to move out to break open the blockade, while the other half of our company stayed back to protect our home base. Our convoy was led by a tank, but alas, it ran over a land mine and was disabled as we got close to the blockade.

The enemy had established well-fortified positions in the mountains above the pass, and our mission was to dislodge and destroy the enemy. The Air Force was giving us air support and dropping napalm bombs and shooting rockets into the enemy's position.

We carried on and came to the blockade, where we met heavy mortar and machine gun fire from the mountain positions. A fierce battle ensued with our troops on the road and the well-entrenched enemy in the mountains. Their mortars were creating a lot of confusion and taking a toll on our company. Our heavy mortars were being fired in retaliation.

We charged up the mountains to dislodge the enemy. This was a new type of fighting—quite different from sitting on top of the mountain and protecting your position by firing down on the enemy as they charged up the mountain. Now, we were the ones being fired down upon. It was extremely difficult climbing up the mountain while the enemy was firing at you. Climb and duck—climb and duck, stop and fire—climb and duck, stop and fire. I charged up the mountain and saw two enemy soldiers jump from their hole and run away. Luckily, I was able to get a clear shot and hit both of them, watching them fall and tumble down the mountain.

The fight lasted for several hours, well into darkness, and our company was scattered all over the area as we chased the enemy into the mountains. The South Korean Marines joined our company, and we all assembled back on the road as the enemy fled. Our company started to pull out with the South Korean Marines, carrying five American soldiers killed in action and several wounded. Also in this battle, we had twenty-eight missing in action, probably killed amid the confusion and darkness.

Bobby McCoun, a Kentucky tobacco farmer, and I were left behind to guard the move back to our base. While the company pulled out, we gave cover to our troops. We waited several hours before deciding it was time to return to our company. However, while we were waiting in the dark, several enemy soldiers were able to get between us and our company. We were trapped behind enemy lines.

We hid in a ditch part of the night and listened to the enemy talking as they were moving out. Needless to say, I was petrified; lying next me in the ditch was a dead enemy soldier. It was a weird feeling lying there with the soldier's dead body touching mine. I swore I would never surrender and was willing to die on the spot if I was discovered—I was not going to be taken prisoner. Thankfully, it was a dark moonless night, and the enemy never spotted us as they moved along the road. Bobby and I crawled along the ditch, through a frozen rice paddy, and hightailed it back to our outfit. That night in the ditch, Bobby and I formed a bond that continued until his recent death. He was a quiet Southerner who liked woodworking; he gave me many handmade gifts from lamps to stools.

The *Stars and Stripes* carried an article about the battle and reported that we had routed 150 enemy, captured 120 mortars, and destroyed a small village where ammunition was stored.

The enemy in retaliation for the defeat at Ambush Alley attacked our mountaintop position the night we got back to safety. I was exhausted from crawling along the ditch and walking back to the base, but when the first bullet whizzed by me, I was ready and willing to give the fight to the enemy.

> 3D DIVISION 27 NOVEMBER 1950
>
> ## 15TH BREAKS ROAD BLOCK
>
> (PIO) A major highway stretching all the way across the Third Division sector, from Wonsan to Tongyang, opened for business again this week when a battalion of the 15th Regiment cleaned out a band of 300 guerrillas who had set up a road block in a treacherous mountain gorge called "Ambush Alley."
>
> In busting through the block, the 15th Infantrymen removed the obstacle which had cut off three companies of the Korean Marines for five days.
>
> Liaison planes from the 3d Division Light Aviation Section had maintained contact with the Marines and had evacuated a number of wounded. Two air drops from C-47's kept them supplied with rations.
>
> The pincer action, in which one company of the Marines blasted through from the west to meet the onrushing men of the 15th, was dubbed "Operation Revenge"—and it was a fitting name.
>
> The Reds had become a harrassing menace, ambushing patrols in the narrow mountain pass.
>
> After "Operation Revenge" 150 enemy dead were counted in the area, and the remaining members of the band had scattered into the mountains.
>
> Four 120 mm mortars were captured, and a tiny village which had held a large cache of ammunition was annihilated.

Freezing in Korea

I am a Minnesota boy and used to snow, but I have never been as cold as I was in Korea. We experienced several snowfalls and blizzards. On patrol, when we went through a small village, we would enter the homes, which were made of paper, mud, and straw, just to get warm. At camp, we kept many fires going, destroying small homes in the area to get firewood. We built fires in fifty-gallon gasoline barrels. Laughing, we made air holes by shooting up the fifty-gallon drums with pistols. It was good target practice.

The temperature was so cold that when you stood to urinate you made sure the wind was at your back since the urine froze as soon as it hit the ground. You had on many clothes so taking a leak was quite an ordeal. As you unbuttoned and unzipped, the cold hit your flesh. Exposed flesh would freeze in a minute. We dug a special foxhole to use as a latrine. It offered some protection. The cold weather killed all odors, thankfully. My war experience has made me appreciate the comfort of a warm bathroom, and I often think of squatting in the frozen, bone-chilling cold.

One never grows accustomed to the discomfort of being cold. Your body gets numb, and you have a hard time moving your fingers. We could not shave, for if you put moisture on your skin, it would freeze. We always carried two pairs of socks— one on our feet and one around our belly to stay dry. When your socks got damp, you would put on the dry ones so you didn't get frostbite.

On the Move

November was a month of holding the top of a mountain, securing roads in the area, patrolling the area, and harassing the enemy while they tried to establish positions. We had the luxury (what a term to use in the cold weather) of developing foxholes and staying in a position for several weeks. Still, we had many patrol duties, and, daily, the enemy tried to retake the mountain or lobbed artillery shells at our position. We were fortunate to repel all attacks. We suffered large losses but were receiving replacements as fast as men were wounded or killed. It was almost a revolving door of young soldiers.

Then, in late November, we received orders to move up north fast. We were going to the Chosin Reservoir to help the US Marines, the Seventh Infantry Division, and the British and Canadian commandos. More than 200,000 Chinese troops had entered the war moving south to recapture the territory occupied by the UN forces.

I was assigned point man for our platoon for the sixty-mile trek through the mountains; it is called point man when you have the honor to be the first up a trail. Baker Company had suffered heavy losses in November during several weeks of combat at Majon-ni, but the worst was yet to come at the Chosin Reservoir.

At this point, I understood General Omar Bradley's famous quote: "The rifleman fights without promise of either reward or relief. Behind every river there's another hill—behind that hill, another river. After

weeks or months on the line, only a wound can offer him the safe comfort of shelter or a bed. Those who are left to fight on, evading death but knowing that with each day of evasion they have exhausted one more chance for survival. Sooner or later, unless victory comes, this chase must end on a litter or in the grave."

CHAPTER SEVEN

FROZEN CHOSIN

By November 1950, the UN forces had defeated the North Korean Forces and controlled all of North Korea up to the Chinese border. China felt it owed North Korea a debt since North Korea supplied many troops to help communist China defeat the Chinese nationalists in that country's civil war. So to pay their debt China entered the war by sending 200,000 highly trained troops across the Yalu River by the Chosin Reservoir. It looked like the Chinese troops would annihilate the 30,000 UN troops. To avoid total defeat, the US troops had to make a successful retreat from the Chosin Reservoir to the port of Hungnam.

The Fifteenth Regiment became part of "Task Force Dog." Our mission was to move up north to the Chosin Reservoir, open up the Funchilin Pass, and help the UN forces move to the safety of the Hungnam port. The battle's main focus was to secure the retreat route against seasoned Chinese troops who controlled the mountaintops.

President Ronald Reagan called "The Chosin Campaign" one of the great battles in US military history. Those of us who were there are called the "Chosin Few," and we experienced the "Frozen Chosin."

I called it, "My Frozen Hell"—the coldest days of my life.

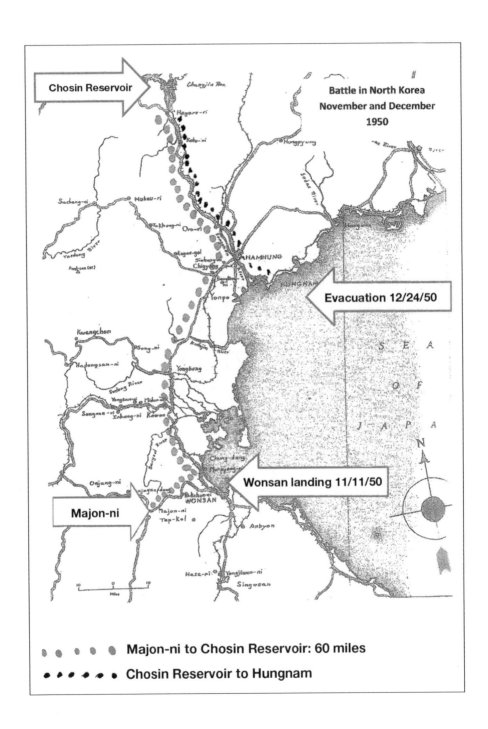

There are tales of a hell full of fire and brimstone and tall tales that you will burn in the fires of hell. I will tell you there is no fiery hell; hell is a frozen wasteland in North Korea. This poem by an unknown author tells it all.

The Day Hell Froze Over

I know I have heard it said
Wait till hell freezes over
It was the day among the dead
It was not flowers and clover
It was the day hell froze over

12/50 way up Korean Northland
Snow and ice were here and there
We heard charge the bugle did command
We fired and fired till none did stand
It was the day hell froze over

December 1950 was three weeks and sixty miles of constant marching, running, moving, freezing, shooting, killing, lack of sleep, hunger, climbing up mountains, sliding down mountains, digging foxholes in rock and ice, and indescribable horror. I was amazed how much a human body can take under the stress of combat and extreme weather. We were walking zombies.

The weather was below zero, but the rifle barrels were red hot, glowing bright in the darkness. You may have heard the phrase, "Wait until hell freezes over." I was there in the mountains of North Korea, and I saw hell freeze over.

Enough cannot be said about the bone-chilling, life-threatening, extreme cold that surrounded us as Korea experienced one of the coldest winters on record in 1950–1951. It never got above zero the entire time I was in the mountains in North Korea. Diesel fuel froze; water froze; canteens of water were kept under our clothes or, if frozen, melted by the fires. My thoughts of combat in Korea always turn to the extremely cold temperature. I fought two things in Korea: the enemy and the cold.

While we were in the mountains of North Korea, fierce winds, constant snowstorms, and below-zero temperatures were the norm. Many days it dipped to thirty to forty degrees below zero. We were outside twenty-four hours a day, on the move, with little time to dig a foxhole for protection. We fought not just the enemy but the extreme cold, the wet, the dirt and filth, the hunger, the constant mountain climbing, the blinding snowstorms, the thirst, the chilling blizzards, and the foul-smelling rice paddies.

Words can never fully describe such endless cold. I was cold the entire time in Korea. To give you some perspective of the comfort level, or lack of, imagine yourself nude in a bathtub full of ice and cold water up to your neck and

With no shelter, I spent a lot of time in my sleeping bag, always ready to fire my weapon. I still sleep with my arms free from any cover.

stay there for several hours. You then may understand cold. I abhor cold weather even to this day. My feet still tingle in the cold weather from frostbite, and I never have a sense of being fully warm. This too I brought back from Korea.

In Korea, I wore wool underwear, a wool shirt and pants, a large parka, and a fur cap made of dog hair that I found in a village. The soldiers looked like piles of clothing with only their eyes showing. Covering body parts was a high priority in the mountains to avoid frostbite, and our gloves had a trigger finger opening.

When not on patrol, I spent a lot of time hunkered down with my feet and bottom half tucked in my sleeping bag and my top half out and ready for battle. It was common to see soldiers with frozen feet, face, and fingers that had turned black. Many troops suffered from hypothermia and frostbite along with me. We captured many prisoners who had severe frostbite. The enemy did not have the warm uniforms we had. The Chinese only wore cotton uniforms, which would get wet and then freeze. They wore rubber shoes and were not well equipped for the bitter cold of the mountains. The Chinese suffered large numbers of casualties due to the weather.

During the Chosin Campaign, I learned what it meant to be cold. My body was one numb mass of flesh.

There was always a strong wind blowing, and it kept swirling the snow, reminiscent of the Clement Clarke Moore poem, "The Night Before Christmas." It was beautiful. It hid the enemy from us and us from them. We were always walking through snow, some waist deep, making it nearly impossible to march rapidly. As we climbed some of the narrow mountain passes, we were never sure if there was solid ground beneath us. I fell a lot but always bounced up and kept moving. No one let down, and I will always remember everyone doing his share. We would tell jokes and count cadence once in a while to warm our spirits.

When we were not moving, we were in our sleeping bags. Since everything froze, we slept with our weapons; my BAR was my bed partner. The oil on the weapons froze. Canned food froze. Every time we stopped, we built fires in fifty-gallon fuel drums to thaw out the water in canteens and the rations but, more important, to try to thaw us out. As much as possible, we kept some cans of food under our clothing to keep them from freezing.

I will repeat, urinating was a real ordeal as you had to keep the wind to your back and the urine would freeze before it hit the ground. Defecating was even worse because you had to find a protected area so your skin would not freeze. When I'm enjoying the warmth of my own toilet in Minnesota, I often laugh to myself and think about freezing my ass off in Korea.

Since we were surrounded, all of our supplies arrived via airdrops in December. The engineers made makeshift runways; until they were overrun, we used them to

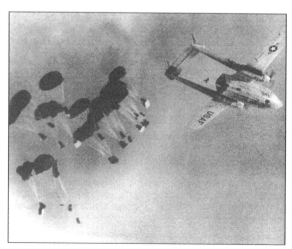

When we were in the mountains of North Korea, we spent a lot of energy fighting the cold and needed a fast intake of energy that the C- and K-rations did not provide. One day the supply plane dropped tons of Tootsie Rolls for us. We gorged on Tootsie Rolls for several weeks. Every time I eat a Tootsie Roll, I think of the cold mountains of Korea.

evacuate the wounded and fly in supplies. I always marveled at the large amount of supplies dropped by airplane.

The airplanes were also used to transfer the wounded, who had to be moved as rapidly as possible. Lying on the ground, they were in danger of freezing.

The battle was fought over some of the roughest terrain during some of the harshest winter weather conditions of the Korean War. The road was created by cutting through the hilly terrain of Korea, with steep climbs and drops. Dominant peaks, such as the Funchilin Pass and the Toktong Pass, overlooked the entire length of the road. The road's quality was poor, and in some places, it was reduced to a one-lane gravel trail zigzagging up precipitous slopes to the four-thousand-foot-high plateau lying south of the reservoir in a mountain range of over seven thousand feet. A narrow gauge railroad went part way and then a cable car incline completed the route. The railroad was destroyed after massive UN bombing raids.

On December 1, our company met up with the Marines and started the retreat to Hungnam. There was no particular day of battle that was memorable. It was fighting every day and night and no end to the number of Chinese. We were constantly in heavy daylong and nightlong firefights and suffered heavy losses. We started down through the valleys with the enemy on the hills taking pot shots at us. I remember firing up at one enemy soldier as he was running on the ridge line, my shot tearing him in half, his head touching the back of his feet.

The killing never ended.

I often thought of the Chinese charges as target practice. There were so many of them, you could not miss when you fired. You hit the enemy, but they kept coming. Then suddenly, it would become quiet, and the charge was over. No mortars, no ar-

tillery, deadly quiet. The Chinese would disappear into the mountains—until the next bugle call.

The United Nations soldiers where brave and made the most of a bad situation in the mountains. As the poet William Blake said, "Great things are done when men and mountains meet." I thought about the stories of Hannibal crossing the mountains and how

Our tired, frozen, hungry outfit following the railroad tracks.

his army suffered. I still marvel today that we survived in the mountains of North Korea surrounded by the enemy.

I recall one night battle against the Chinese. Some came on horses, charging down the mountains blowing bugles. They herded women and children in front of them to set off the land mines. Flares, fired from artillery and dropped from planes, lit up the sky. The flares hung in the air on parachutes, casting an eerie light as we watched the bodies torn apart by the land mines. I can never forget the senseless killing of the women and children.

Another night during a vicious battle, I recall that Pop Davis was wounded by an artillery shell and was praying aloud for a chance to see his wife and children again. He was one of the older soldiers, about thirty or forty years old, and he was always talking about his children and showing us photos of them. Such a proud father. I held him, and he died in my arms. His God did not save him. I lost faith in God as I saw soldier after soldier killed or wounded as they prayed to live.

Anything in front of us was an enemy. Shoot to kill was my motto. I experienced a variety of emotions during this time, ranging from pure hatred to love, from fear to bravado, from religious belief in a deity to nonbelief in any god. I came to the reality that regardless of a soldier's belief when the bullet is meant for him he is dead. I saw men die while asking their God to save them and give them the power to kill the enemy. In war, there is neither a God of salvation, a God of destruction, nor a God of love. There is only the brotherhood. The brotherhood, where fellow soldiers believe in each other and share a love that cannot be explained in any other way other than to say, "I am willing to give my life to save my fellow soldier." That is the pure emotion and religion of combat.

When you are willing to give your life for your buddies, it is hard to see your friends being killed around you. I never got used to it. Again and again, I discovered tears frozen on my cheeks as I watched a friend die. The tears froze and dropped off, leaving the sadness.

Baker Company moving up to the Funchilin Pass.

This poem by Donald Chase explains my feelings.

Killed In Action

We met in Korea you and me
Was in that land death set you free,
I remember when you died, my friend,
An incoming round your life did end.

Tears blurred my vision when you were killed.
Upon that hill your blood was spilled.
Brought back home, you now sleep alone,
Date of death upon your stone.

The years have come and gone
It seems they just flew by.
It's called, "America's Forgotten War"
In which my friend did die.

Our airplanes controlled the air. Day and night, there were bombing raids. Marine Corsairs kept the mountains on fire with napalm bombs. The air power kept the enemy from overrunning our positions. Just as soon as they had the sheer numbers to overtake a position, we were on the move south again. I was interviewed in the Pacific edition of *Stars and Stripes* and was quoted as saying, "Our air power keeps the enemy miserable all the time."

As we battled, their body count mounted. You could not count them because the body parts were entwined. My head was spinning with the large number of dead bodies all around us. Several times artillery shells would hit the dead bodies and throw body parts all over the area. It was not uncommon to see severed limbs and burning bodies lying around the battlefield. It is hard to find the words to describe this kind of carnage.

The assault on December 5, 1950, was a typical battle. It started after midnight. The first we knew that the battle was going to take place was the noise of a land mine exploding; it had been placed in front of our perimeter about five blocks away. Then several bugles started to blow. Artillery and mortar fire started falling into our perimeter. The ground was exploding in front of us. Sometimes the mortar shells would set off the mines, showering us with dirt, snow, and ice.

The damage a mortar shell can do is indescribable. The shell leaves a big hole, where once there had been level ground or a tree. Big rocks and boulders were shattered and flew around like deadly missiles. When an incoming shell came whistling in, you ducked into the best cover you could find. We held our positions against the barrage and stayed in our foxholes waiting.

We called in for air and artillery support. I could see the explosions in front of our lines from the light of flares as artillery sent high-flying parachutes hooked up to flares to light the area. Airplanes were dropping napalm bombs and strafing the area. The hills were on fire, but the Chinese kept coming, running down the mountain. They looked like an endless sea of ants. They charged, and I saw bodies on fire and body parts flying through the air. There was a terrible stench. It was Chinese soldiers burning.

While the air support did their work, I kept firing my BAR in sweeping motions and watched bodies fall in front of my position. My barrel was red hot and glowing in the darkness. I threw snow on it and listened to it sizzle. I stopped to toss several grenades and then pulled a couple of clips from my belt and started firing again, mowing down the enemy. One Chinese soldier jumped right in front of me, so close his stomach touched my gun barrel as I fired. They were stepping over their comrades' bodies trying to get to us.

When a bugle sounded, they stopped and blended into the landscape. We kept vigilance because we knew the bugle would call them again and they would reappear as before, and they did. More men. Attacking and attacking. Soon my foxhole had bodies piled in front of it, and I had to move dead Chinese away from my foxhole to have room to fire my weapon.

I heard the screams of some of my fellow soldiers, who had been hit. They were calling for a medic. I was in a trance and could only look at the enemy in front of me. I again threw grenades while several bandoliers of ammunition were brought to me. My trigger finger seemed frozen in position. My ears felt as if they had lost all hearing from the loud noise of my weapon. Napalm bombs lit up, and a wall of fire spread in front of me. Chinese soldiers caught in the napalm screamed. This stopped them for a second, as they could not advance through the blaze. I continued to fire and knew we had held.

A bugle sounded. All was quiet. The Chinese ran back up the mountain, and the planes continued strafing and napalm action. The artillery continued. In the morning, I was on patrol to survey the carnage. Daylight showed hundreds of dead Chinese soldiers. Some were whole, some burned, some in parts. We searched them even though some were still smoldering. The smell was awful, but it was cold and they would freeze to slow the decomposition and control the smell.

We were making progress on our retreat to Hamhung when suddenly we were stopped because the Chinese had destroyed a bridge over a 1,500-foot gorge by the Funchilin pass. We were in trouble. We could not move to safety, and the Chinese could mobilize all of their troops against us. However, the engineers repaired the bridges with treadway bridge supplies dropped from airplanes. It was remarkable to watch the large pieces of equipment attached to three or four parachutes float down through the sky and land in the right place. I always admired the pilots and the engi-

Picture of dead Chinese soldiers after a battle and a snowstorm that covered up all the dead bodies.

Digging in and waiting for the Chinese to attack.

neers who built that bridge. The bridge was repaired, and we fought our way on foot through Hellfire Valley to the safety of Hamhung.

I repeat: December 1950 was a month of daily fighting, killing, freezing, marching, and hiding. Pure hell. The entire month melted into one daily battle against an enemy well trained to kill us. Eventually, after nearly a solid month of killing and being shot at, what was left of our company made it to the Hungnam perimeter on December 23, 1950.

Frozen Hell

Bodies of dead US troops.
Frozen bodies were common in December, and I saw this scene daily.

Frozen Hell

The dead were blessed, loaded on trucks, and
brought out with us. We were fortunate to bring
back the majority of our dead. Below right: Grave
registration—GIs tagging the dead soldiers.

Chosin Battle

Fifteenth Regiment moving toward Chosin Reservoir in late November.

Airplane strafing and dropping napalm bombs. Notice all the fire.

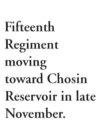

Typical wave of the enemy charging up a hill.

Chosin Battle

In the North Korean mountains, we never had enough clothes to keep out the cold.

Chosin Battle

Chosin Battle

Typical scenes of the retreat from the Chosin Reservoir to Hungnam. It was below zero the entire time in December.

We had to take the Chinese prisoners through the ambush with us. The Chinese fired on the prisoners as well as us. It was complicated, and to our credit, we never killed anyone who surrendered.

Chosin Battle

A common scene during combat was fires in the distance caused by Corsairs dropping napalm bombs.

Chosin Battle

Pictures of the Hellfire Valley bridge that was destroyed. There was heavy fighting here. Our troops were stalled at this point while the bridge was repaired.

This scene says it all. We honor our fallen heroes. We walked with honor and dignity out of the Frozen Hell as our dear ones rode on the truck draped with American flags.

Aftermath

While not a victory in the classic sense, the withdrawal from the Chosin Reservoir is revered as a high point in the history of the US Army and US Marine Corps. In the fighting, the UN troops effectively destroyed or crippled seven Chinese divisions, which had attempted to block their progress.

Our losses were staggering from the enemy-withering fire and the extreme cold. Thousands of soldiers on both sides suffered from frostbite. Marine losses in the campaign numbered 836 killed, 2,000 wounded, and 500 missing in action. US Army losses numbered around 2,000 killed, over 4,500 wounded, and over 4,500 missing in action. Precise casualties for the Chinese are not known but are estimated at 35,000 killed and 70,000 wounded.

Upon reaching the port of Hungnam, the veterans of the Chosin Reservoir were evacuated as part of the largest amphibious operation to rescue UN troops from northeastern Korea.

Everyone who survived the Chosin campaign is a hero.

CHAPTER EIGHT

HUNGNAM EVACUATION

Exhausted Baker Company troops arrived at Hamhung, a city ten miles from Hungnam. Our mission was to hold the perimeter while the rest of the UN troops and refugees were loaded onto ships sitting in the Hungnam harbor. I vividly recall a tender moment when a wounded marine said, "Thank you," while being carried on a stretcher toward the docks.

Our last engagement in North Korea during the retreat was when we were ambushed near Hamhung by the pursuing Chinese Eighty-ninth Division, which the Third Infantry Division repulsed with little difficulty. We had great naval and air support. Sitting in the Hungnam harbor were battleships, cruisers, destroyers, and aircraft carriers. They laid a barrage of horrendous firepower into the mountains. The Chinese as much as they tried could not overcome the barrage of the heavy guns. The airplanes from the carriers gave constant cover. It was explosion after explosion—nonstop boom, boom, boom, boom. You could hear the sixteen-inch guns from the battleships as they whooshed overhead and a little later there was the boom from the explosion. My ears rang from all the noise.

While the UN troops were being loaded for evacuation from North Korea, we did have the luxury, if that's what you would call it, of having a foxhole to call our own.

Oddly, I watched the Chinese stand on the hill, wave good-bye, and then duck back into their foxholes. They knew they had forced us out of North Korea, but I had no feelings of defeat. I was just happy to get out of this hellhole.

I was one of the last soldiers to leave; I helped guard the engineers as they planted huge boxes of explosives. When we left, we blew up everything. During the evacuation, there were 193 shiploads of men and materials—105,000 soldiers; 98,000 civilians; 75,000 vehicles; and 350 tons of supplies that were loaded and taken back to South Korea. I left Hungnam on December 24, 1950, at 1700 (5:00 p.m.) on the *USNS Collins* troop ship and was greeted as a hero by the Navy. They were slapping me on the back and yelling, "Glad to see you."

My best Christmas present that year was a hot shower. I had worn my filthy combat clothes from November 11, and they were full of blood, dirt, and stuff I don't want to think about. I didn't know if I could ever get clean, let alone warm. I stood in that shower, soaping and rinsing, soaping and rinsing. I still remember the thrill of the hot water running over my body and the warmth starting to seep through me. The Navy seamen kept bringing towels and juice to drink while I dried off. They treated me like a king. I loved the Navy guys for their kindness. They gave me real food prepared by a cook and pies, many pies. Maybe that is where I got my desire to eat pie. Anytime we were hungry, we could walk down to the mess area and ask for food, real food, not C-rations.

We left the port and sailed to South Korea. North Korea faded into the background, and I was preparing for the next adventure. We had an opportunity to write home and were given a card to send home.

The troops received a note from President Harry S Truman. It was sent to General Douglas MacArthur at the Third Infantry Division Headquarters and said, "I wish to express my personal thanks to you, Admiral Joy, and General Almond and all your brave men for the effective operations at Hungnam. This saving of our men in this isolated beachhead is the best Christmas present I have had."

Christmas Greetings from The Far East

CAN DO

15TH Infantry Regiment
25 December 1950

We sailed from Hungnam to Pusan and spent Christmas Day on the ship, celebrating with the sailors, hot food, hot showers, clean clothes, and a lot of camaraderie. On December 28th, we left the ship and boarded trucks to move up north. The battle was going to begin again.

Hungnam Evacuation

Refugees in the port of Hungnam asking for safety from the enemy.

US troops arriving to load up on ships at Hungnam. There was
a constant flow of refugees and US troops going to the docks. All
day you could hear the battleships in the harbor shooting their
big guns and the shells whistling overhead.

Hungnam Evacuation

Above: The Third Division, my division, are the last soldiers to leave
Hungnam. The last of the evacuees (I am in there somewhere) wave and
cheer on the deck of a landing craft as it pulls away from Hungnam beach,
Christmas Eve 1950. Below: A hell of a Christmas present for
North Korea as Army engineers blow up the docks of Hungnam on
December 24, 1950.

CHAPTER NINE

RECONQUERING
SOUTH KOREA

We evacuated from Hungnam on December 24, 1950, sailing away on the *USNS Collins.* My vacation of luxurious warmth, good food, and a daily shower lasted three days. We unloaded at Pusan, South Korea, on December 26, 1950.

We were immediately loaded on trucks and moved up to the front lines. On December 30, 1950, I was back in the combat zone. The Chinese had moved south of Seoul, and we were the guys to stop them.

I spent New Year's Eve 1950 shooting off fireworks (incendiary bullets) from my BAR. All along the line, you could hear soldiers shouting, "Happy New Year!" The Chinese attacked us on New Year's Day, and the battle ended on January 2, 1951. We stopped the Chinese advance, and Baker Company was on the offensive.

Prior to moving into position to attack a hill south of Seoul, our company commander arranged for all of us to send home a Happy New Year's telegram. It gave me a feeling of warmth to think of celebrating a new year back home, perhaps next year, with a big Sonsalla dinner and a bowl of oyster stew.

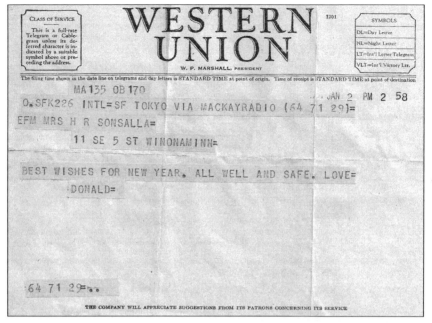

We were encouraged to make contact with home whenever we could because we often went for weeks without the opportunity for communications.

In Pusan, I found out I was in a new war. We had orders to move out and advance toward Seoul. We were moving north fast as we advanced along the line. It was a change from Chosin, where we were retreating and the Chinese were chasing us. We were now chasing the Chinese.

We were in an area with roads and cities not just villages. This is where I got my first taste of urban fighting. Instead of shooting from a foxhole, I found myself shooting from buildings. Our bombs and artillery had raised hell with the cities, and what we missed, the Chinese hit with their mortars and artillery. Many cities were totally destroyed.

Comrades in Arms

On this new assignment, I had a chance to meet soldiers from other countries. Soldiers from Belgium were attached on our right side. They were a well-trained outfit and made history by conducting a dramatic bayonet charge, which frightened the enemy.

I met soldiers from Turkey and Greece. They were all friendly, and we celebrated with them. I was in awe the first time I met a Turkish soldier. I was sitting in my foxhole on the top of a hill, and I saw a person approaching our line. He was holding a Thompson submachine gun above his head yelling, "Me Turk, me Turk." We held our fire and someone went down to the man and led him through the land mines to our position. We had a language problem, but via radio we were able to contact a Turkish unit and a translator. Two squads, along with my squad, escorted the soldier back to his unit. We were met by Turkish soldiers with marvelous handlebar mustaches who showered us with handshakes and back slapping. We all stood around a huge bonfire, keeping the translator busy with several conversations going at once.

The Turkish soldiers were fierce and feared. They cut off the ears of dead Chinese soldiers as a souvenir of their exploits. They loved to patrol alone at night, adding to the strings of Chinese ears dangling from their belts. The Chinese were afraid of

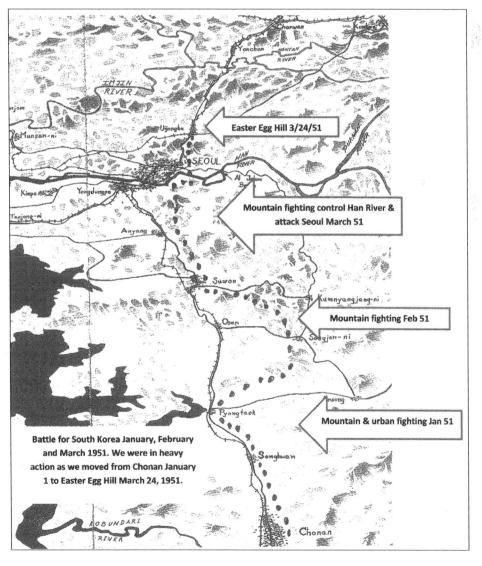

Easter Egg Hill 3/24/51

Mountain fighting control Han River & attack Seoul March 51

Mountain fighting Feb 51

Mountain & urban fighting Jan 51

Battle for South Korea January, February and March 1951. We were in heavy action as we moved from Chonan January 1 to Easter Egg Hill March 24, 1951.

In January 1950, Baker Company moved to meet the Chinese. My morale was high as we were on the offensive and ready to kick some ass.

the Turks because of this propensity for mutilation. The Chinese, I was told, feared that having their ears removed would keep them from reaching heaven as a whole person. If you wanted to punish a Turk, just deny him a chance to go on night patrol alone, hunting Chinese ears.

Not only did the Turks take ears, they took heads as well. I saw Chinese heads tied to the hoods of the Turkish Jeeps. Visiting with the Turks was like being in a spooky movie, and I marveled at the experience.

The Turks carried swords on their belts, and when they pulled out the swords, they cut their hand a little. I in turn joined them and cut my right hand a little on their sword. The translator said, "We are bonding together as blood brothers." That night I became a blood brother to a Muslim, but, in combat, we were all blood brothers.

Whenever I had a chance, I would hitch a ride on a tank.
It sure beat walking when I was dog tired.

Later the Turks brought out some awful tasting liquor; contrary to what you hear, Muslims in combat drank liquor. We danced around the fire and laughed. I discovered that they make big fires to attract the enemy and invite the enemy to shoot at them. Then they know the enemy's location and can go out on an ear-cutting mission.

The Greeks were also great soldiers and also had the habit of taking Chinese heads and tying them to the hoods of their Jeeps. We walked through the Greek outfit one night on a mission and stopped to share some of their fire. Via a translator, they invited us for a drink of some of their favorite liquor. It didn't taste as bad as the Turkish stuff. The Greeks went into their foxholes, changed into white skirts, and grabbed our hands, and we danced around the fire. I still laugh when I think of that night—a bunch of dirty GIs dancing around holding hands with Greeks in skirts.

As I think back on it now, I realize that I thought nothing of the Turks and Greeks taking enemy body parts as souvenirs. It shows how unfeeling combat makes an individual.

Poor Refugees

The sadness of war hit me every time we passed through a village, and I saw the massive damage wrought by troops and artillery and the refugees begging for food and help. Moving through the refugees was always a danger because some of the enemy would pose as refugees.

One of the ways that the poor civilians survived in the cruel war was to keep two sets of flags: a South Korean flag and a North Korean flag. Flag exchanges were typical scenes in villages. One day when we were on patrol, we entered a village, and as soon as the civilians saw us, they took down the North Korean flag and raised a South Korean flag. As we were leaving the village, I looked back and saw them

So many refugees were trying to escape the horrors of war. I sympathized with them but had to move on to the battle.

89

already replacing the South Korean flag with the North Korean one. Such is the cruel fate of civilians in wartime.

One sad scene I observed, and still shudder when I think of, was of a *mama-san* (the name we gave to the women) walking through the checkpoint line maintained by the MPs. She was wearing an A-frame, the Korean version of a backpack. The MPs checked the A-frame and found a grenade. They pulled the pin, sent her on her way, and hit the dirt. The grenade exploded, leaving the woman a mass of blood and body parts. It was hard to accept the death of another innocent victim of the war.

During the American Civil War, General William Sherman said, "War is hell." He forgot to add—not only is war hell, but also the recollection of war is hell to a combat veteran. During night terrors, I visit hell and see the stares of the enemy as I killed them. I watch an innocent woman explode in front of me.

Urban Fighting

Two of my lifelong buddies, Larry Long and Marvin Ashby, joined our company in January 1951. Marvin from Indiana was the jokester, and Larry was the storyteller. Larry, a tall, lanky black from the South, had a hard time writing so I wrote his letters home for him. I was his first white friend, and he tended to stay close to me. Marvin, on the other hand, loved to go on patrol and sneak into towns to catch the enemy by surprise. He came home with a Silver Star and an injury that haunted him for years. He was shot in the face with a .50 caliber gun and was unable to close his right eye for forty years. Both Marvin and Larry received Purple Hearts for their valor in the Korean War.

Forty years after the war, I received a letter from Marvin Ashby. He and I had shared a foxhole in Korea. When I was wounded on Easter Egg Hill, Marvin was behind me and had to keep charging up the hill. I was a bloody mess. Marvin lost contact with me. And then, forty years later, a letter (via the Veteran's Administration) arrived, written by Marvin. He was wondering if I was the Minnesota soldier who was in the foxhole with him and wounded on Easter Egg Hill. He also inquired if I remembered the day we brought a couple of South Korean women to our foxhole.

At every Baker Company reunion, Marvin apologized to Verna for telling about the Korean girls in the foxhole. The story is simple: We were on the line south of Seoul and getting ready to recapture the city. Marvin and I went on patrol to a small village and were warmly greeted by the mayor who spoke English. The mayor invited us in for tea. When his two daughters came in, the mayor introduced them to us, and to make a long story short, we invited them to see our foxhole where the American soldiers lived. The four of us walked up the hill and crawled into our sleeping bags. It was a cozy fit. In reality nothing happened because the other soldiers made such a fuss that the girls became frightened and we had to take them back to the village.

I was becoming adapted to house-to-house fighting and hated the idea that the enemy was right around the corner. Night patrol was never any fun because at night sounds travelled and you could hear people talking. They were speaking Chinese or Korean, and I had no idea what they were saying. Were they friend or foe? I couldn't tell until I saw them. Were they wearing uniforms or civilian clothes?

During one terrifying experience while on patrol in a small village, I identified the enemy not by sight but by smell. I call it my garlic story. I was sneaking (I know it is hard to imagine me sneaking) around the corner when I smelled garlic and froze on the spot. The Chinese and Koreans used a lot of garlic to spice up their food. It seeped from their pores, and they reeked of garlic. Quietly, I pulled out my combat knife, swung my BAR out of the way, and waited. I had to kill this enemy soldier without making a sound.

The Chinese soldier coming around the corner never knew what hit him. I grabbed him with my left hand over his mouth and lifted him into the air while I stuck my knife up under his chin straight through to his brain. I heard the crunch of the knife entering his head, and blood gushed from him all over my clothes. I held him tight, his face touching mine. I could not see his expression; it was too dark. He struggled for just a few seconds. I held him like that for about a minute to make sure he was dead, then I laid him down on the ground and signaled for the rest of the patrol to follow me. We continued, scurrying behind the buildings to a dike and got back to our position. I get the chills when I think of that enemy's face touching mine in death and always turn the lights on when it is dark. He may be around that corner, and I don't want a repeat of that.

According to military records, we attacked the Chinese in an offensive maneuver and charged up a hill by Towo-Li on January 12th and suffered heavy losses. That's the way January went—attacking the Chinese and taking back territory that we had given up. Morale was high, and sometime during that time I was made a corporal and was serving as a squad leader.

February was a repeat of January. It began on February 1st, with us charging up a hill, bayonets fixed, yelling and swearing at the Chinese. As I ran firing my BAR, I had an odd feeling; I felt invincible on that hill. I felt as if no one in the company would get hurt. I was wrong. The Chinese fought back. Some of our men fell. Then, suddenly, the Chinese stopped, crawled out of their holes, and started to run away. It was a wholesale surrender. I walked along rows and rows of captured Chinese soldiers. It got to be routine: We charged, we exchanged gunfire, and then the Chinese surrendered en mass. During January and February, we frequently heard "I surrender" in a Chinese accent.

Celebrating the capture of so many Chinese, we established a perimeter on top of a hill. On February 2, a fresh Chinese company charged up the hill. We held,

Chinese soldiers surrendering in rice paddy.

hitting the Chinese for four days until we broke their offense and sent them on the defense. The Chinese were on the run but stopped at Tong-ni long enough to organize reinforcements and raise hell with us again, as we advanced and they retreated. It was tough fighting, and we had major losses in early February.

On February 21 and 22, we marched through heavy rain, snow, and a hail storm. Roads were flooded. We were up to our hips in mud and then it froze. Temperatures plummeted from the low thirties to ten degrees in one day. It was rough trying to climb up the hills. Tanks and trucks were mired on the roads. The good news was it slowed down the Chinese as well, and we were able to hit them hard as they tried to organize to get back north over the Han River.

I experienced a new cold—getting wet and having my clothes freeze on my body. You can bet we loaded those fifty-gallon drums with wood and made roaring fires to thaw out.

The first part of March we were on the south side of the Han River and exchanging artillery fire with the Chinese. We had to keep under cover when we heard the Chinese mortar rounds coming in. My ears still ring,

This photo of a dead Chinese killed during a battle in March was sent to me by a Baker Company buddy.

and I can hear the loud explosions of the mortar and artillery shells in the back of my head. Weird feeling.

Assigned to be a sniper, I sat on the south side of the Han River shooting at anything that moved in Seoul. It was an unfair advantage for me. I was constantly hitting the enemy troops as they tried to establish a defensive position on the bank of the river. I felt no sympathy for these soldiers as I lined them up in my sights and pulled the trigger. It reminded me of shooting squirrels in Minnesota.

I had no compassion; I had become an animal thirsting for the kill.

We were always on the move, going as fast as the elements allowed.

On these marches, we sang the Third Division song:

I wouldn't give a bean
To be a fancy pants Marine
I'd rather be a
Dogface soldier like I am

I wouldn't trade my old ODs
For all the Navy's dungarees
For I'm the walking pride
Of Uncle Sam

On Army posters that I read
It says, "Be all that you can"
So they're tearing me down
To build me over again

I'm just a dogface soldier
With a rifle on my shoulder
And I eat raw meat
For breakfast ev'ry day

So feed me ammunition
Keep me in Third Division
Your dogface soldier's A-okay

I remember my birthday. I was getting ready to attack Hill 291
and thought, "What a hell of a birthday present charging up a hill
in Korea freezing my ass. Happy birthday, Don."

There were countless enemy troops killed. I shed tears when I found dead
GIs mixed in the mess of bodies. We carried many dead GI bodies from
the battlefield after the medics indicated there was nothing they could do
to save them.

US Army photo of the Fifteenth Regiment in March 1951 moving up. We were always on the move, going as fast as the elements allowed.

We tried to stay on the trail and not step into the shitty rice paddy.

One of the major problems we faced in Korea was getting supplies to the front lines. There was always a hill or mountain to climb and always snow in the way.

If we were not fighting to take a hill, we were marching to another position to engage the enemy. I did a lot of walking up the damn hills and mountains of Korea. They are not kidding when they say, "All you do in the infantry is march, march, march."

I will share an interesting snowstorm story. In February, we were on the attack chasing the Chinese and getting ready for a large assault on a hill. As we were moving up, a huge snowstorm hit us. It left over ten inches of wet, heavy snow. Everything stopped. We had orders to bunk down because of limited visibility. We crawled into our sleeping bags, and I fell asleep. When I woke up, I was covered with snow, as was everyone in our company. The snowstorm had silenced the enemy, as well. They too were buried in snow. The snow gave us a day of peace and quiet. It was grotesque to see the white snow stained with blood. I still see the blood-stained snow during snowy days. It took us a full day to walk up the hill through knee high snow to get in position to attack the hill.

Stories from the Lighter Side

February and March 1951 were days and nights of constant fighting south of Seoul. Yes, it was horrific, but there were also lighter moments. One way to keep morale high in combat is to look at the experience, if possible, in a humorous way. The following events in some cases are frightening, but I looked at them, at the time, with a light heart.

The rice straw pile story occurred one day when I was on patrol with a squad of six (five GIs and one ROK soldier). We were scouting a small twenty-hut village, going from house to house looking for ammunition or enemy supplies. Suddenly, a large number of Chinese soldiers came up the rural road led by a Russian tank. The enemy spotted us immediately. There was a burst of machine gun fire from the tank as well as cannon fire. Bullets were coming in rapid bursts striking the ground. We ran looking for a place to hide. I saw a rice straw pile about ten feet high. I jumped behind it. While lying there getting ready to fire my BAR, I heard the bullets whistling though the rice straw. I thought, "Sonsalla, you are one dumb Polock; straw can't stop bullets."

Laughing, I rose and dashed behind a hut and then to a ditch. The other squad members all made it to the ditch. Our squad returned the enemy fire. I saw two Chinese soldiers about fifty feet away running along the hill toward the village. I fired my BAR and hit the two Chinese soldiers in the chest and watched as they fell backwards from the force of the bullets.

We left the village to go back to our lines, running along the ditch. For some reason, the Chinese did not follow us. It was one of the oddities of the war because they had us outnumbered. We called for air support, and thirty minutes later the airplanes were flying over the village while we were climbing the mountain to get back to our position, A Marine Corsair flew over and dropped napalm bombs on the Chinese. Sad to say, the village was left in burning ruins after the airplanes had finished bombing.

The wild boar story happened while I was on a patrol with my squad in the hills of South Korea, and I spotted what I thought was a pig running in front of us. There were many domestic pigs in the villages, and I thought this was a pig that got loose. I shot the pig with my BAR and hit him with all twenty bullets in my clip. The pig collapsed with most of its head shot off. It turned out to be a wild boar. We carried the boar back to our position. There, a good old Southern boy named Corporal Mabry Hall from the swamps of Louisiana knew how to butcher animals. He was a tough soldier and always whittling wood—when he wasn't fighting the Chinese or cooking up boar. We built a large fire and dined on roasted pork.

Just a few days later, I was sitting in my foxhole and saw a deer run in front of our position. I shot the deer in the head. Luckily, it did not land on a mine. We retrieved the deer, built a fire, and had roast venison for supper.

It is handy having several hunters who know how to skin and dress animals, as well as cook them, when you go to war.

Although we received a daily four-can beer ration while in Korea, we found ways to stretch our supply of alcoholic beverages. We put the beer outside in the below-zero temperature. Since the alcohol did not freeze, we could pour the alcohol out and use it in other drinks. GIs become very creative in combat situations. We were always seeking ways to get liquor. We sampled the rice liquor that we found in the villages, but I did not like it. It tasted like sour milk mixed with vinegar. We also were the proud owners of a traveling still. GIs from the backwoods of Louisiana had experience in making homemade alcohol and kept us supplied. How they did it, I will never know, but we ended up having a traveling still. They made alcohol from rice and potatoes that we mixed with water and snow. The taste was awful, but we drank it.

Once while searching through the belongings of dead Chinese soldiers, I removed a red star from a soldier's cap. I was surprised when I turned it over and found that it had been made from a Hamms beer can. Hamms was a popular beer in Minnesota, and in a funny way, it reminded me of home. I carried it for a long

time as a souvenir, but left it in Korea in my sleeping bag when I was wounded. All of my stuff was left on the line.

This is one of the few pictures (taken in March, I think) that I have of me in Korea. I had several rolls of undeveloped film in my sleeping bag, but when I was hit, they stayed in Korea, and I have no idea what happened to the camera or the film.

To keep up our morale, we had a traveling blackjack game. We kept a record of winnings in a cigar box. I have no idea who was ahead. When I was wounded, the cigar box and records stayed in Korea. I asked Marvin once about the cigar box. He said, "I lost track of it when I was wounded."

Little did I realize that as a Boy Scout in Minnesota, where I did a lot of camping, that I would end up in Korea living outside in the worst weather, 24/7, without the comfort of a tent and only the night sky for cover. This picture tells a story about my living conditions in Korea. I'm on the left, sitting with two of my foxhole buddies: Marvin, who was wounded in action, and Dick, a tugboat operator in World War II who was called back from Reserves and killed in action in Korea on Easter Egg

Hill. I am wearing heavy snow pac boots (rubber and waterproofed), several layers of clothing, a parka, and a fur cap. In the background, you can see numerous rice paddies, hills, and another GI position.

There is an empty cardboard box, which held our C-rations. We have wood by our position ready to build a fire to keep warm. I am getting ready to deal a hand of blackjack, a favorite pastime. We are sitting on a rice straw mat as protection against the cold ground. We have a traveling cigar box and scorecard to keep track of winners and losers. The whole time I was in Korea I was never paid. My money was sent home. From November until March, I never used any money.

George Wright was my platoon commander in Korea in January, February, and March. He replaced our previous platoon commander, who was wounded in action. George was an enlisted man in World War II and received a battlefield commission. He was a soldier's soldier. George would always lead a charge up the hill. He was one of the first to attack and earned the Silver Star in Korea for leading us in a bayonet charge in February. He was brave and much admired.

George delivered his short, simple orders in a Southern accent. He stressed that the important thing was to get home alive. He was a natural leader.

George always seemed to know the latest rumor or what was happening behind our lines. One day he asked Marvin and me to come to his foxhole and pointed out that there was a load of liquor in the back lines by the artillery group and our company could use a drink of real stuff. Marvin and I got the message. We went on a midnight requisition (a military term for stealing something), found the liquor truck unprotected, stole it, and drove it to the bottom of the trail where several Baker Company soldiers helped unload it. Then we drove it back. For awhile, we had scotch and other whiskey with our beer and homemade booze. Several days later, some MPs visited our line inquiring if we had heard of any liquor in the area. Of course not, we said. From that day on, George Wright could do no wrong for Baker Company.

I recall the day I fed beans to a dead Chinese soldier. There was heavy fighting for control of the hill. When there was a lull in the fighting, I observed the scene. Dead frozen Chinese soldiers in grotesque positions were strewn all over the area, the bodies so thick you could not walk without kicking a body out of the way or stepping on one. It was time for a luxurious C-ration dinner. I stopped for a lunch break. I could not find a place to sit so I sat on the body of a dead legless Chinese soldier. He was lying on his back with his gaping mouth and wide-open eyes staring at the sky. I opened a can of beans and franks, one of my favorites, and suddenly, I had an urge to feed beans to the dead man. Slowly, I dropped several beans into his mouth. It was a surreal moment. I felt nothing. I was numb. Combat does that to you.

As I think back on it sixty years later, either it was an act of hatred or maybe in some small way it was one soldier's tribute to another soldier. I don't know which. I do know that many times, after a battle, I talked to the dead Chinese soldiers.

Surviving in Korea

It was near zero degrees, a frigid, snowy January day in 1951, and our company was fighting the Chinese near Seoul. We had orders to take a hill at night. I hated the night fighting with the flares lighting the sky in an ominous flickering, wavering light. It was a surrealistic scene. I was leading our squad up the hill on a narrow path when a voice called out, "It is safe; come up here."

I knew we were the front squad and answered, "Who is this?"

The voice responded, "It is the Fourth Platoon."

That was a big mistake because the Fourth Platoon was heavy weapons and never in front of an advancing squad. I led two men, maneuvered behind the voice, and found a Chinese machine gun nest waiting for us. We were fifty yards away, and I could see two Chinese soldiers. I unloaded my clip of twenty rounds at the one by the machine gun hitting him in the head and watched as his head disintegrated. Exhilarated that I had killed another enemy, I thought, "That will teach you."

Marvin Ashby shot the second Chinese. A third Chinese, who was hidden, yelled in English, "I surrender; please do not shoot." I talked to the surrendered Chinese soldier, who was an older fellow, spoke excellent English, and had been educated in the United States. Other American soldiers joined us, and the prisoner was taken to the rear.

One of our most prized possessions in the company was a shortwave radio. We could receive stations in America. We listened to a country western station from San Francisco that played a lot of Hank Snow and his famous song, "I'm Movin' On": "See that big eight-wheeler coming down the track. It means your true lovin' baby ain't coming back . . ."

We also listened to Japanese stations and knew some of the songs. Later while in the hospital, I bought a radio and again listened to "Movin' On."

DONALD R. SONSALLA

Some of the Fellows I Met

We had nicknames for enemy and friend. We called the enemy Gooks and Chinks. I was called Tank because I was big. Other nicknames were Pecker Nose, Young Bill, Old Bill, Killer, Bobby I, Bobby II, Mac, Marv, Larry, Pops, Ray, Dick, and the company commander who was called the Old Man.

Robert Spanbauer was a tough combat soldier and always willing to volunteer. We all teased him about being the youngest kid in our outfit. One day the company commander received a notice that Robert was only sixteen years old and sent him home just before the battle at Easter Egg Hill. That probably saved his life.

We had twins in our outfit—the Twigger boys—who were always scrounging food. They had enormous appetites, and every time we took a village they loaded up on the rice and kimchi (Korean sauerkraut). We all knew they were sixteen, but the Army never found out.

After a battle, when I had time to think, I often wondered what war was all about. I thought about the hardships but mostly about the bravery of the men in Baker Company. This poem by an unknown author expresses how I felt:

> Often when I sit alone and twilight fills the sky,
> I find myself recalling scenes from other years gone by.
> Memories of Korea still clutter up my head,
> Those dreary days and hellish nights, and my friends long dead.
> The many hills we fought through, which never seemed to end,
> And all the while the fear inside, of death around the bend.
> The clashes with the enemy, who sometimes fled away,
> But, for every hill we won, someone had to pay.
>
> Maybe one was lucky, when a bullet found an arm;
> For a little while at least, you were safe from harm.
> My mind recalls the icy weather, when diseases took their toll,
> When frozen feet were common, from winter's numbing cold.
>
> The trench line with its bunkers and grimy faces there
> Where if you were observant, you saw a burned-out stare.
> The pathway from the trenches that led to no-man's land,
> A torn and barren piece of ground, destroyed by human hand.

Always there were those who fell to never arise,
And to this day, I still can see the shock in startled eyes.
These vivid pictures locked inside, although they do not show,
Never seem to leave my thoughts no matter where I go.

During February 1951, we had established a line south of Seoul and dug in by the Han River. I recall one dark, moonless, foggy night when three of us were assigned to take a small rubber raft across the river on a scouting mission. The Han was a large river, the size of the Mississippi at Winona, Minnesota, about one block wide. The Army had experimented with two-man rubber boats that didn't work; a wooden boat was too heavy to carry so we ended up with a six-man rubber boat that held three guys with equipment. The river, partially frozen with large ice chunks,

Left: Prisoners brought back from across the Han River. Bottom: A soldier with a BAR using a tank as cover on the Han in February.

We patrolled the Han River and established control of the area.

was open, and it was possible to launch a boat. In black face and carrying weapons, we quietly paddled against the current and were about half-way across the river when we bumped into something in the dark—another rubber boat.

It was a Chinese patrol.

No words were spoken. Both boats turned around and went back to shore. One hour later, artillery from both sides of the river started pounding.

The following night we tried again and completed the patrol. We found an area that the Chinese had failed to secure. It was a good spot to launch an attack and attempt to retake Seoul.

The Chinese made one last charge as they loaded in boats and paddled across the Han. Our artillery and air force cut them down before they reached our side of the river. It was sad to watch all the bodies torn up in the river. What a loss of mankind.

Korea Units Fight 88% Of The Time

SAN FRANCISCO.—The savage pace of the war in Korea was emphasized this week by 6th Army headquarters here in releasing figures showing that U. S. divisions rotating men to the States have spent an average of 88 per cent of their time in actual combat.

Highest percentage of any of the divisions is that of the Army's 3d. Although it was credited with less time in Korea than the others (162 days), 155 of them were spent in the line for a percentage of 95. Figures included operations up to April 22.

Lowest percentage (77) was held by the 1st Marine Division which spent 170 days in combat of its total of 220 days.

The breakdown follows:

Commands	Pct. of Days in Combat	Total Days in Korea	Days in Combat
3d Inf. Div.	95	162	155
24th Inf. Div	92	296	274
25th Inf. Div.	89	287	256
1st Cav. Div.	87	278	243
2d Inf. Div.	84	266	223
7th Inf. Div.	84	220	186
1st Mar. Div.	77	220	170

The 65th Regimental Combat Team of the 3d Infantry Division had 40 days of combat in Korea before the initial action of the 3d Division and was in Korea 51 days prior to the arrival of the division. (Not included in table above.)

The 1st Marine Brigade was in Korea 42 days and had 33 days combat prior to the arrival of the 1st Marine Division. (Not included in table above.)

Note that the Third Division, our division, had the most time on the line or in combat.

★ ★ ★

Prior to taking one hill in March, we were supported by the Twenty-ninth British Brigade Tankers. They came rumbling down the road in huge Churchill tanks, making a lot of noise. The few shots being fired at us from a distant hill were bouncing off the tanks. We were hiding behind the tanks for protection. Suddenly, the tanks stopped, rocking to a halt. The tankers climbed out of the tanks elegantly dressed in their clean uniforms. We were dirty and unshaven and looked like derelicts. They started a fire with Sterno cans and invited us to tea. It was a strange tea party. When the Brits finished their tea, they got into the tanks and turned the cannons toward the hills. They laid down an awesome barrage. The shooting from the hills stopped. I guess the tankers knocked them out. Needless to say, I was impressed by the Brits' professional demeanor.

I am taking a break before we go into battle for Easter Egg Hill on Easter Sunday. I am the one on the far left not facing the camera. All the other guys in this photo were either wounded or died in Korea. This gives you an idea of the cost of war.

★ ★ ★

We crossed the Han River and began fighting for control of the city of Seoul. Luckily the air power, our snipers, and our artillery had forced the Chinese to withdraw from the edge of the river. The engineers did a wonderful job of building a pontoon bridge across the wide Han.

There was some light fire from machine guns and mortars coming in as we crossed. I don't remember anyone from the company getting hit while we crossed the Han and entered Seoul.

Seoul in 1951

The fighting was light when we entered Seoul, since most of the Chinese had left to establish positions in the hills north of Seoul. On March 21, we moved north of Seoul to the Uijongbu area. We were about to engage in Operation Courageous, the conquering of Hill 337 (Easter Egg Hill).

CHAPTER TEN

THE BATTLE OF EASTER EGG HILL AND MY MILLION-DOLLAR WOUND

Before we attacked Hill 337 (Easter Egg Hill), we fought through Uijongbu, a bombed-out town that had mostly been destroyed on March 23, 1951. As we entered Uijongbu, there were few buildings standing. We were shooting and hiding in partial buildings. Contrary to what you see in the movies, bullets tear through wood, and a wooden wall does not protect you from military rifles.

The official military title for the Easter Egg battle was "Operation Courageous." Simply stated, the 187th Airborne Division was to attack Hill 447 to the north, the Sixty-fifth Regiment was to attack Hill 155 to the west, and the Fifteenth Regiment was to attack Hill 337 thus trapping the enemy. Hill 337 was important because whoever controlled it, controlled the surrounding roads in the area. The enemy had a lot of time preparing for this battle, building fortifications with artillery and mortars supporting them, but we were determined to dislodge them.

It was a well-lit night as we left Uijongbu, and I could see Easter Egg Hill, our target, in the distance. The full moon was shining brightly that evening as we

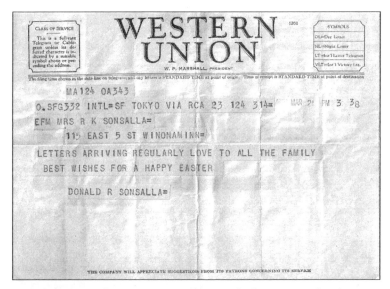

It was ironic that we were getting ready for a major battle on Easter. The company commander gave everyone an opportunity to send a telegram home wishing our families a happy Easter. Here is my telegram message.

Uijongbu was almost totally destroyed by the time we took the city.

Street fighting in Uijongbu. The Chinese were moving out, and we were moving fast from building to building.

prepared for battle with an enemy, well entrenched in the mountains. The red color of the moon reminded me of the blood that would be spilled on Easter Sunday.

As we moved along the road in single file toward our destination, my company for some strange reason was marching on the right side of the road rather than both sides. Suddenly there was a familiar whistling in the air and we all yelled, "Incoming!" We hit the dirt on the right side of the road, as the enemy shells exploded on the left side. If the shrapnel didn't kill you, the noise would scare you to death. Luckily no one was hurt.

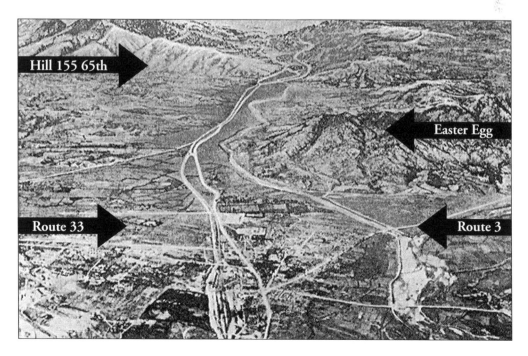

We continued along the road, and were about to cross a bridge when machine gun fire started coming at us from a hill to our right. The gunfire (incendiary bullets) appeared like fireflies in the distance. I recalled an infantryman telling me, "If you see where the incendiary bullets are coming from and you use them, they can see where you are."

We ran under the bridge, splashing through the Changnung River as .50 caliber bullets zeroed in on us. I can still hear the sound of those bullets as they hit the cement, rocks, and water. Luckily no one was hit while we ran under the bridge and toward a dike at the base of Easter Egg Hill. There was a lot of yelling and someone yelled, "Let's take that damn hill before they get us."

We dug in by a large dike and started laying fire on the enemy. The enemy was lobbing mortars at us, but they were falling short and hitting the rice paddies in front of us. The mortar explosions were getting closer to us, and we had to make our move.

We had to cross the rice paddy, which was covered with ice and water, and if you slipped off the edge (as I did), you were one shitty, smelly mess.

I was firing my BAR, and some of the GIs were throwing grenades as we crossed the paddy.

We had orders to charge up the hill. There was a large twelve-foot bank in front of the hill by the rural road. It was impossible to climb. I moved to the right and saw a cemetery. There was a small path leading up the hill by the cemetery.

1. Changnung River. 2. I ran under this cement bridge when the enemy opened fire from a nearby hill.

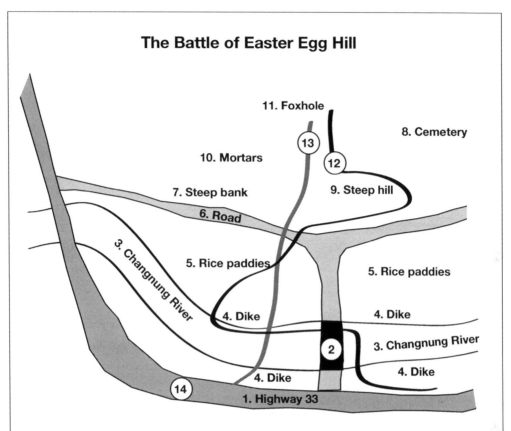

The Battle of Easter Egg Hill

11. Foxhole

8. Cemetery

(13)

10. Mortars

(12)

7. Steep bank

9. Steep hill

6. Road

3. Changnung River

5. Rice paddies

5. Rice paddies

4. Dike

4. Dike

(2)

3. Changnung River

4. Dike

4. Dike

(14)

1. Highway 33

1. Highway 33.
2. Bridge I crossed under with machine gun fire hitting us.
3. Changnung River, where I rinsed my wounds in dirty, shitty water.
4. Dike. We laid heavy fire on Easter Egg Hill from this position.
5. Rice paddies that were a mixture of ice, water, and manure.
6. Small ungraded rural road.
7. Steep 12-foot bank, which prevented a full frontal assault on the hill.
8. Cemetery with stone markings and religious symbols.
9. Steep part of the hill from the cemetery to the mortar positions under heavy small arms fire.
10. Heavily fortified mortar positions.
11. Camouflaged foxhole where the Chinese soldier hid. He leaped from this hole and threw the grenades at me.
12. My path attacking the hill. I climbed the dike, ran through the rice paddy, climbed the bank by the cemetery, hid behind the gravestones, ran up the steep bank, ran to a mortar position, shot two Chinese, and continued up the hill. Then the Chinese soldier jumped up and threw the grenades at me. Boom. I fell down.
13. Path after I was wounded. I scooted down the hill, tumbled down the bank, crawled through the rice paddy and over the dike, and fell into the river.
14. Tank picked me up here and took me to a stretcher jeep.

I was firing my BAR and some of the GIs were throwing grenades as we crossed the paddy.

Elements of the Fifteenth RCT, Third Infantry Division, fire upon Communist dug-in positions on a hill near the village of Uijongbu, Korea.

I stayed off the path because of land mines, instead dodging from tombstone to tombstone firing my BAR. I saw a couple of Gooks above me and fired at them, knocking out two of them by a mortar site. I got to the fortified mortar site and emptied a clip into two more Chinese in the hole.

I continued up the hill to the next position.

Suddenly, a Gook jumped up from a hidden foxhole right in front of me.

I saw a string of hand grenades coming at me. I fell to the ground firing and hid under my helmet. I heard and felt a large explosion.

When the grenades exploded, my mind registered a pure white flash.

After the explosion, I tried to get up to jump in the hole and get the Gook, but I could not stand.

I was in shock. I had no pain. What was the problem?

I looked down below my waist and saw that my clothes were saturated with blood. I knew I had to get out of there. Again I tried to stand up and could not. The shrapnel had hit me in the thighs, both knees, and my feet. It had torn the back muscle in my left leg and caused severe nerve damage. Of course, at the time, the depth of my injuries didn't register. I just knew I couldn't walk, and I was angry at myself for letting the Gook get the drop on me. I started to scoot down the hill backwards, laying fire in front of me.

Bob Kent, who was behind me, jumped in the hole and shot the Gook that got me. He yelled, "Get back to the medics." Bob was from Georgia, a good dependable soldier who was always preaching and praying. He often asked God to give him the strength to kill.

I continued to fire. I tried again and again to stand but could not. I could only crawl. I had lost control of my legs and was seeing double. I continued to fire as I fell down the bank. I crawled through the stinking rice paddy, swearing with every

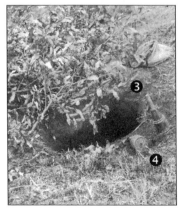

1. Mortar. 2. Trench. 3. Foxhole. 4. Grenades.
Bottom right: Medics unloading wounded to be taken to a MASH unit by helicopter.

move I made. I still felt no pain. As I reached the dike, I fell over it and into the cold river. I thought I could wash away the blood. I watched, as if in a trance, as my blood turned the water red.

I was yelling for a medic. Just then the Chinese mortars hit us, and at the same time, our artillery fell short. Mortar shells were hitting the water, the explosions bathing me in mud. I was in a haze passing between consciousness and unconsciousness. My mind was in a fog, and it was as if I were watching a movie with no control of my actions. It was a weird feeling, like having a dream and never waking up.

When I opened my eyes, I saw a medic leaning over me. I was being loaded on a tank, which took me to a Jeep equipped with a stretcher. As I said before, the medics were the heroes of the war.

I had sustained what we called a "million-dollar wound," a wound severe enough to get me back to the States but not so bad that I was leaving any arms or legs in Korea.

4. Grenade

1. Sleeping
bag and
ammo carrier

2. Food pouch

3. Burp gun

Here is a picture of a Chinese soldier in his winter uniform. The Chinese tied several grenades together when they threw them to deliver maximum damage.

CHAPTER ELEVEN

MASH UNIT

I felt no pain and was floating in and out of consciousness as I was loaded on a tank and taken to a MASH unit. I awoke and found I was in the Spanish-speaking Puerto Rican Sixty-fifth Regiment MASH unit. I knew no Spanish and vaguely recalled that someone offered me a drink of whiskey from a bottle. I remember drinking some whiskey and passing out again.

When I woke up, I was lying next to a soldier. I was receiving a live blood transfusion because I had lost a considerable amount of blood. I was in and out of consciousness and vaguely aware of being hooked up via a tube to a body next to me and their blood flowing though my body. I did not know if my donor was male, female, gay, straight, a minority, or of what religious denomination, but at that point I didn't really care, this individual saved my life. I wish I knew the name of this volunteer so I could thank him or her personally. I was at the MASH unit but unconscious after the blood transfusion, and I have no recollection of what happened to me at the MASH unit. I recovered to semiconsciousness when I was being loaded on an airplane. My VA medical records show that the MASH doctors had operated on me and took out a lot of shrapnel, repaired bone and muscle damage, and cleaned up my wounds.

An interesting story about the mentality of a combat veteran: I had been in combat January, February, and March, eating just C-rations (canned rations) and K-rations (dried rations) and no fresh fruit. As I was being loaded onto a C-47 hospital plane heading for a hospital in Japan, I was floating between consciousness and unconsciousness. I was in a fog and had a fever. An Army nurse

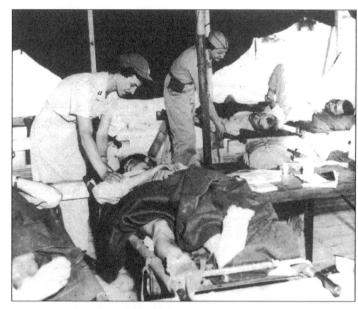

This is a typical picture of a MASH Unit. I was treated at a unit like this while waiting to be transferred to Japan. I remember little of the MASH unit since I was in and out of consciousness most of the time.

asked if she could do anything for me. Several ideas floated through my head. One, I asked if I could send a letter home. I wrote a short one-sentence note that I was doing well and had a slight wound; the nurse said she would see that it was mailed home. My second request, and don't ask me why, was, "Could I have an orange?" At that point, I passed out again and woke up over a week later in a hospital in Japan.

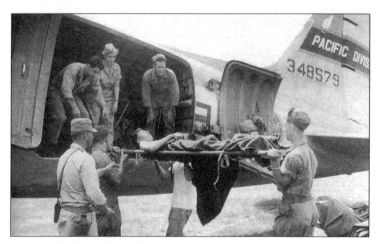

One of the last things I remember is being loaded on an airplane similar to the US Air Force C-47 hospital plane shown above.

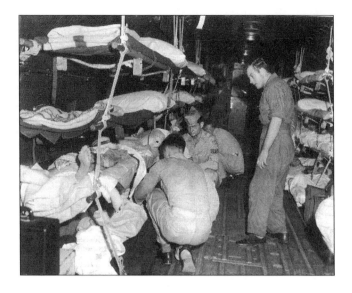

Notice of Wounded in Action

After I was wounded and evacuated to the 141st Army Hospital in Japan, my parents received the following telegram from Major General Edward F. Witsell.

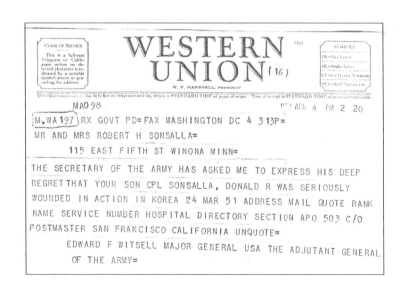

Corporal Donald R. Sonsalla, above, 20, son of Mr. and Mrs. Robert Sonsalla, 115 East Fifth street, is recuperating in Japan after being seriously wounded in action in Korea. He saw action in both North and South Korea, having been in combat since November. In a letter to his parents, received Monday, Corporal Sonsalla said he had leg injuries. He enlisted April 3, 1950, and flew to Korea in October. His address is: R.A. 16329321, Ward X, 141st Gen. Hosp., A.P.O. 1005, in care P.M., San Francisco, Calif.

★

The Winona Daily News ran an article about me after I was wounded in Korea.

CHAPTER TWELVE

HOSPITAL IN JAPAN

After the flight from Korea, I woke up a couple of weeks later at the US Army 141st Hospital, which was located in an old converted Japanese naval air base in Fukuoka, Japan, on the island of Kyushu in the southern part of Japan.

I was in a large ward with forty hospital beds, side by side. For the first couple of weeks, I was in and out of consciousness, loaded with morphine. My legs were bandaged, and one was tied up to a stand above the bed. I could not walk or get out of bed. I had a severe case of blood poisoning and infection from the shrapnel embedded in my body. Between the shrapnel wounds and blood poisoning, I was running a high fever. I had a hard time trying to wake up due to the morphine shots, which I received in my hind end every four hours.

In addition, I recall some discussion about the fate of my left leg. At one time, the doctors wondered if it could be saved. The leg had turned black and was swollen. In 1951, President Truman (my hero) signed a presidential order that any soldier wounded in battle had to give his consent, if possible, before any amputation could take place.

Thankfully, I was conscious when the Army doctors, who did a great job, were discussing the problem with my left leg. They wanted to amputate. I said, "I would rather die than lose my leg," and refused to sign off on the amputation. In the end, they were able to knock out the blood poisoning and infection with massive penicillin shots in my butt along with the morphine.

While I was recuperating, I listened to a shortwave radio. No idea where I got it, but I listened to a station from San Francisco and kept up on the news. (This is maybe where I acquired my love for listening to and watching the news.) I remember hearing Hank Snow's "Movin' On," one of our favorite songs in combat. As I listened to Hank sing, I thought of the foxholes where I heard his music and how it boosted my morale.

As I was healing, the shrapnel formed pimples on my legs and thighs. A nurse from Pennsylvania, a short gal whom I would describe as rather chesty, would come in, squeeze the area where the shrapnel was coming to the skin, pop it out, and cleanse the wound. During night rounds, if you were lying in bed with an erection, she would give it a whack, laugh, and say you had better get well so you can get into town, but I was defenseless and could not get out of bed. So town was not an option for me. I hated the bedpan scene and was determined to get well.

While lying in bed, I read every book they brought me. I also did some sewing and embroidering on dishtowels. Anything to keep my mind busy. I talked with the guys, and we told war stories, many of them funny. The ward was filled with soldiers with serious wounds and several amputees. All of them were brave, and none complained about the situation.

I vividly remember the first day I got out of bed and could use a wheelchair. I was like a kid with a new toy, wheeling all over the hospital. Several times the guards would have to bring me back as I would try to get out of the fenced-in compound. I knew I was on the mend and enjoyed wheeling around, feeling the sun on my face. One day I talked a male aide into wheeling me outside the fenced area to a small Japanese bar where we had a beer. When we returned to the gate, the MPs just turned their backs to us, pretending they didn't see us sneaking back into the compound.

I still laugh every time I see a wheelchair and think of my exploits during my recovery. I was not going to be stopped from enjoying myself while

Looks like I am sleeping on the job.

122

confined to a wheelchair. We had wheelchair races and placed bets. I played Ping-Pong, football, and softball in a wheelchair. The Japanese aides would wheel me to town for a price, of course: cigarettes. It is hard to explain the euphoria I felt when I could leave the wheelchair and use crutches. That led to new entertainment: crutch fights with the other guys.

What a thrill to know I could again use my legs. The pain was there and the wounds would break open and bleed, but I could walk. No longer was my Ping-Pong game limited to the wheelchair. Now I could play Ping-Pong with crutches. Yes, I fell many times but laughed because I could get up by myself.

Then came the day when I walked for the first time without crutches and could use a cane. What a thrill.

Top: I'm mobile with crutches (leaning on the building). Notice my bandaged leg.
Bottom: At last, I'm free—no crutches.

The entire hospital staff was wonderful and experts in dealing with severely injured soldiers. They kept our morale high and always were in good spirits. There were down days when a soldier would die, but the sadness was short lived, being replaced by a patriotic feeling that they had served well. It is hard to explain the feeling of both pride and sadness when faced with the death of a fellow soldier.

It is interesting to note that one of the nurses who helped me while I was in Japan was Faith Wehinger. I found out she was from Kellogg, Minnesota. We talked about Minnesota and what was happening in the States. She often changed my bandages when I had blood poisoning. I remember the bandages had a vile odor, but she would always look at me with a smile and say, "Oh! It looks so much better." She was good for me and kept me posted on the Minnesota news. Little did I know that we would meet several years later at my wedding reception in Kellogg. Verna and I were standing in the wedding reception line, when along came Faith, my nurse from Japan, to congratulate us. We recognized each other, hugged, and laughed. What a small world.

After three months in the hospital, I was getting around well and most of the bleeding had stopped. I then suffered a setback. I got yellow jaundice and lost all appetite. I was served six milkshakes a day along with medicine. Eventually, the yellow jaundice cleared up. The doctors speculated that I received it from a live blood transfusion at the MASH unit.

My greatest claim to fame was that I was in bed with gorgeous Jennifer Jones, the number one movie star in 1951. She was the sexpot in the movie *Duel in the Sun*. While I was in the hospital, a USO tour came through, and Jennifer Jones stopped by my bed (I could not get out of bed yet at that time). She sat on the bed, held my hand, and asked, "How are you doing, soldier?" or words to that effect. It was a big thrill. I am sure Jennifer's touch helped my healing process. In addition, I saw Bud Abbott and Lou Costello, the world-famous comedians, when they visited our ward. Lou Costello shook my hand and said, "Thanks for your service."

Red Cross worker, name unknown, did a wonderful job. She made all the guys feel good.

There was a lot of camaraderie in the ward, and I made friends easily. One of my friends was a tall, dark guy with an East

Top: Jose Ramunz served in the Sixty-fifth Regiment and was wounded the same day I was. Right: I'm enjoying a snack on my hospital bed.

Coast accent named Donald Levi from Washington, DC. He came from a wealthy background, had grown up with house maids and chauffeurs. He planned to go to Georgetown University. We played a lot of cards for money, and Don was always losing and borrowing money from me. I was making money because one of the aides in the hospital and I worked out a deal where I supplied him with cigarettes and he took them to town to sell. We split the money. When my hospital stay in Japan was over, Don and I shook hands and said we would get together after the war.

Another friend I made in the hospital was Jose from Puerto Rico. We were Ping Pong opponents. Jose was movie star handsome and liked to brag about the beauty of his homeland. He invited me there, and I invited him to experience the snow in Minnesota.

I was lucky to meet a Japanese English-speaking hospital aide when I was walking around with crutches. She was about forty, five feet tall, bossy, and had been educated in the United States before World War II. The hospital staff allowed her to take the patients on trips to Nagasaki, where the atomic bomb hit in 1945. I went on one of the train trips to Nagasaki with two other patients. It seems the Japanese and US government wanted everyone to see the damage that an atomic bomb can do. About 30 percent of Nagasaki, including almost all of the industrial district, was destroyed by the bomb. Nearly seventy-four thousand people were killed and a similar number injured.

We toured Fukuoka in an Army Jeep driven by a soldier and then boarded the train for Nagasaki. I was surrounded by Japanese civilians, and they all bowed on the train when I went past them. I recall mountains in the distance around the city. Nagasaki was a bombed-out mess, even though the blast was over five years ago. I think they kept it in ruins just to show the world the power of the atomic bomb.

When I became adept at walking with a cane, I got shipping orders to board a naval hospital ship. We left port and set sail for the United States on a cold, windy day. I was to report for temporary duty at Fort Belvoir, Virginia, for outpatient treatment at Walter Reed Army Medical Center in Washington, DC.

I was going home, but my war wounds would continue to bother me for years.

In the fall of 1952, I had to go to the VA hospital in Minneapolis to be treated for blood poisoning when the shrapnel caused an infection. I returned to the hospital again in 1960, when shrapnel worked out behind my knee cap.

I had an opportunity to visit Fukuoka, the closest city, and a
Japanese photographer took these pictures just before I shipped
home. It was my last day in town.

These photos were taken during my last week at the
hospital in Fukuoka, Japan.

CHAPTER THIRTEEN

BACK IN GOOD OLD USA

I took a Pacific cruise on a hospital ship back to the USA. During the fourteen-day trip, I was seasick but still spent some time on the decks. I watched GIs playing craps, money piled on the decks beside them as they threw the dice. I didn't play but enjoyed watching the game.

At one point we were sailing through the Aleutian Islands, with Russia on our right side and Alaska on the left.

When we arrived at San Francisco, I boarded an airplane, walking with a cane at the time. I met my parents and sister, Joyce, in Chicago for a fourteen-day leave before reporting to Virginia. The first thing we did was go to a bar by the Chicago airport. I ordered a beer, and the bartender asked for my ID. All I had was my dog tags. The bartender said, "I can't serve you because you have no ID, and the law says no liquor if you're younger than twenty-one."

I grabbed him by the shirt and told him, "I just came back from Korea all shot up; I'm gonna come across this bar and wreck the place with my cane if I don't get my beer. Call the cops if you want."

My mind was still in Korea, and I was full of anger from my war experiences. I was ready to kill the guy. The guy said, "No problems, take it easy." I cooled off and reminded myself that I was home in the USA. That was the last physical confrontation I had. I was really afraid of what I would do after months of killing. I was in for a real adjustment. To make a long story short, I got my beer, and he thanked me for my service. Several guys in the bar bought us drinks. My mother said, "Donnie, I never saw you so angry; lucky, the guy served us."

We drove back to Winona, and I had fourteen days of meeting relatives. I never talked about combat to any of them. My folks had no idea of what I did in Korea other than a couple of fun stories. I bought a 1946 Buick and drove to my new assignment. I loved that big car. I was assigned to Fort Belvoir by Washington, DC, as an outpatient and received treatment at Walter Reed in DC. I was in a temporary company of recovering soldiers and had light duty. I was officially assigned as a high-speed steno because I knew how to type. My duties were to take minutes in a court-martial of officers. Luckily, there were no hearings so I really had nothing to do.

I spent a lot of time in DC, taking in the sights, practically living in the museums. I met up again with my friend Donald Levi, a millionaire. He was my host, and I traveled with him and his Jewish friends. They had money and paid all the bills. When we were in the hospital in Japan, Don kept borrowing money from me and said he would pay it back when I visited him in DC, and he did.

I was lucky to have a wide circle of friends in DC. I met Shorty, a combat vet from San Juan who was an outpatient at Fort Belvoir. He introduced me to several Puerto Ricans; I marveled at their dancing in the night clubs. He also invited me to his home for meals. There I met his gorgeous wife, Juanita, who had a temper and scared me a little.

Occasionally, I would go into town with Bad Bobby, a tall, thin, black combat vet. I was one of the few whites in the clubs that Bad Bobby frequented, since there was still segregation in 1951. Bad Bobby and I talked about the race situation in Virginia and DC, but it didn't keep us from socializing together. We never had any trouble except once when some kids called me a "nigger lover."

One of my good friends was Babe Lilla, a muscle builder from Winona. He was stationed at the Marine barracks in DC and was on the honor squad. We hung out in a local country western bar called the Wagon Wheel across the street from the Marine barracks. There I took some friendly teasing from the Marines about being in the Army.

One day when I was driving back to Fort Belvoir, I saw a guy sitting on a small bridge fishing and said to myself, "Only Virgil Schaffner from Winona would do that." I stopped, and it was Virgil. He was attending sheet metal school at Fort Belvoir. Of course, I took him to town to meet Babe, and we went to the Wagon Wheel.

We were having a beer when a knife fight broke out. That was the last time Virgil went to town with us. I still laugh about that.

One friend who was a good guide for all of the sights was Sue, an elderly Red Cross worker at Walter Reed who arranged trips for the "wounded warriors" (the name for outpatients)—sightseeing tours to plays and musicals. The Red Cross workers took good care of the troops.

My stay in DC was short, but long enough for me to lose my senior class ring from high school. Here's how it happened. I was in uniform in the lobby of Walter Reed Hospital when I saw a short, cute, blonde nurse named Jane. We exchanged hellos, and I made a crack that if she weren't an officer, I would ask her for a date.

"I'm a civilian," she said. She lived in Alexandria, Virginia, with her parents.

And that was the beginning. We dated, became good friends, and exchanged class rings. When I was discharged, we broke up, but Jane never returned my ring.

I went home to Winona after being discharged and started my life as a civilian. I attended Winona State, where I met Verna. We married and had two daughters: Debbie and Judy. Both our daughters went to Winona State and met their husbands there.

Debbie, an underwriter for an insurance company, married Erv Neumann, a school principal in Charlotte, North Carolina, and had two children. Their daughter, Dana, received her undergraduate degree from Elon College then went on to law school at the University of Tennessee. She is in the US Army now. Lee, our youngest grandchild, attended the University of North Carolina Chapel Hill and is employed in the business world.

Judy owns a management consulting company. She married Greg Lissick, an underwriter for an insurance company, and they live in Vadnais Heights, Minnesota. They have two sons: Grant, who has a degree from the University of Wisconsin Eau Claire and works for the Hennepin County Sheriff's Department, and Joel, who has a degree from Minnesota State in Mankato and works in business. Grant is married to Jen, a pharmacist, with degrees from the University of Wisconsin La Crosse and the University of Wisconsin Madison.

I am proud of my family and their accomplishments.

I received an education in the Army. I was introduced to many cultures and diverse populations. It gave me a taste for learning. In fact, learning and helping others to learn became a passion. Eventually, I earned a PhD in educational psychology and educational administration. I worked for the St. Paul Public Schools for forty years.

CHAPTER FOURTEEN

EASTER EGG HILL REVISITED

The South Korean government instituted a Korean War revisitation program where they paid all expenses which included airfare, a week's stay at a five-star hotel, and a tour of the battlefields in Korea. This program was in appreciation for our service in saving South Korea from North Korean oppression. I took advantage

This is the foxhole where the soldier hid. He had it covered with branches. He tossed back the branches, stood up, and threw the grenades at me.

of this program and was fortunate to have some free time with a guide and driver to visit the areas where I had been in combat and especially Easter Egg Hill. The visit ended with a huge banquet at which time the vice president of South Korea awarded each veteran a Republic of Korea service medal.

My visit to Easter Egg Hill in 1985 brought back all the memories of that fateful Easter Sunday 1951. The foxholes, trenches, and mortar positions are still there. I had one mission: to walk to the top.

I walked from the cemetery to the mortar position and stood in the foxhole. I could feel the spirit of the Chinese soldier who had thrown the grenades at me. I paid respect to his courage and reveled in the thought that I had survived and could actually stand in the spot where I was wounded. It was a moving experience, and I stood transfixed for over an hour. The guide asked if I was okay. I was back in March 1951 charging up the hill again.

I walked all over the hill and looked at trip wires that were used to set land mines. Later, I found out that there were warning signs throughout the area: "Live ammunition. Stay away." But since I could not read Korean, I ignored them. My visit to the past was complete. I had made it to the top of Hill 337.

View from the top of Hill 337. I finally made it to the top.

Easter Egg Hill Revisited

Top: Mortar positions. Top left: A monument honoring
Chinese soldiers killed on Hill 337. Top right: Sign warning of
live ammunition.

On my visit, I talked to a Korean, who lived in this hut at the bottom of Hill 337. He had been in the army and had observed the battle of Hill 337.

Baker Company Reunions

As I mentioned earlier in the story, forty years after the war I received a letter from Marvin Ashby. That letter was the catalyst for the start of Baker Company reunions. Marvin had contacted several other Baker Company veterans, and twenty-two years ago, eight of us met in Little Rock, Arkansas. There were tears and hugs and a feeling of warmth as we were able to express our joy over seeing each other again after so many years.

From that first meeting, we established a yearly Baker Company Reunion and met at various Army posts every year for twenty years. Perhaps this was the first time our spouses, as they overheard bits of our conversations about various battles, had a real understanding of what we had gone through in Korea.

Sadly, the number of attendees diminished from a high of more than thirty at reunions to only six at our last meeting at Fort Sill, Oklahoma. Death and illness had taken its toll, and meetings were no longer feasible. Those of us who remain still keep in contact via e-mail, letters, and telephone. I was fortunate to be able to visit my close foxhole buddies, Bobby Grodhaus, Bobby McCoun, and Marvin Ashby in their hometowns until their deaths. I miss them but still cherish their memories and can visualize them in the foxhole defending our freedoms.

CHAPTER FIFTEEN

REFLECTION

In war, there are no unwounded soldiers.

Post-traumatic stress disorder (PTSD) is a medical condition that results in a person experiencing a traumatic experience in his life and then reliving the experience via flashbacks. It results in various behavior patterns. I have flashbacks that sometimes are like movies and other times just a flashing picture that disappears. Since the war, I have a dislike of the dark and, if possible, always have a night-light on. It stems from night patrol. I always tell the soldiers I killed "good-night" and talk to them for a second and then I am free to sleep. On occasion, a huge night terror wakes me, and I am in a major firefight. I push this flashback away by simply getting up and walking around, reading, or watching TV—anything to bring me back to the present.

The worst part of PTSD is not only do you relive the horror and the fear of war, but you lose your foxhole buddies, the guys you came to love, again.

I found poetry written by combat veterans of the Fifteenth Regiment helps to express my feelings. It may sound trite, but it is hard to talk about this portion of my life without shedding some tears and again experiencing the sheer terror of war.

The Real Forgotten War
By Donald Chase

The guns of war are silent now
Yet I can hear them still
I see the faces of the dead
I guess I always will

They say that time will ease the pain
Can make a man forget
Though almost sixty years have passed
I see the carnage yet!

Korea was so long ago
Or was it yesterday?
I hear the screams, in torturous dreams
O let me wake I pray

The awful sounds of exploding rounds
Still ring within my ears
So many dead and dying
Yet there's no time for tears

Positions that are overrun
With fighting hand to hand
How many did I kill, dear friend?
I hope you'll understand.

At last the fight is over
The endless night is through
We won the fight for that hill
But those who lived are few.

So when it's time to judge us, Lord
And weigh just what we're worth
So many died, so few remember
We served our hell on earth.

Memories of Korea

Some of my closest foxhole buddies—all holders of the Purple Heart—each in their own way have shared with me their feelings about the Korean War.

Marvin Ashby, a PTSD and reformed alcoholic whose face was disfigured by shrapnel and machine gun fire, wrote poetry expressing his emotions. Marvin and I were brothers in war. When my foxhole buddies pass away, a little bit of the history of Baker Company and the Korean War passes away with them. I salute them as the real heroes of the war.

The Men of Company B
15th Regiment - 3rd Division

More than forty years have passed us by
When first time we had met.
But in September we will meet again
In a time that has been set.

Several men will meet this day
To laugh and cry and say,
"I've missed you friend.
How have you been
In these times we have been away?"

When I ask them of their families
And their eyes begin to glow
I will know that you have blessed them Lord;
Just as you have blessed my family so.

I know that too we will speak about
The pains we all did share.
About the loss of these fine young men
And the heartache that's still there.

And of these men we want to thank you God
Up to the very end.
That in our lives you gave to each of us
A very special friend.

Let's not forget in our times of prayer
When we look to you above
Fail to give our praise to you dear God
For your name means and teaches love.

By
Marvin L. Ashby
9-13-93

Bobby McCoun's tribute to the Korean War: "All gave some. Some gave all."

Bobby McCoun from the hills of Kentucky shared one night in a ditch with me surrounded by Chinese troops and dead bodies next to us. We bonded that night. Bobby was a craftsman and sculpted a wooden figure "Lest We Forget." Also here is a newspaper article about Bobby.

Bobby Grodhaus, a fellow BAR man, loved the Third Division and sent me some Easter Egg battle souvenirs he made.

Bobby Grodhaus made a wooden figure and in his own way told the story of Easter Egg Hill: a cracked egg symbolic of our battle for Hill 337 on Easter Sunday.

Bobby McCoun Plays It Cool

WITH 3D DIV—It had been a long, hard day and Company B of the 15th Regiment had fought well and with success and now the day was almost over. The hill was virtually in American hands. Virtually.

One lone, last foxhole stood in the way. Its occupant apparently had decided not to vacate, come hell or high water.

Darkness was coming on and the men of the 1st Platoon were cursing an enemy who would not quit, even when he was licked. It all seemed so futile for that one last foxhole to continue to rattle out death when the rest of the hill was quiet.

The 1st Platoon put in a call to the 2d Platoon to ask if the latter could approach the Communist position from the rear. The message wasn't clear on the 2d Platoon end of the line.

So someone in the 2d sent Cpl. Bobby A. McCoun, of Lawrenceburg, Ky., off to the 1st Platoon to see what the message had been.

McCoun made his way through the darkness until he arrived at a foxhole in which one occupant crouched, automatic rifle in hand.

"Is this the 1st Platoon, bud?" queried McCoun.

It wasn't. Instead, it was the one Chinaman who had held up the 1st Platoon. But he was through, particularly when faced by an enemy who would walk right into his position. He threw up his hands.

The hill was secure, the day's work done.

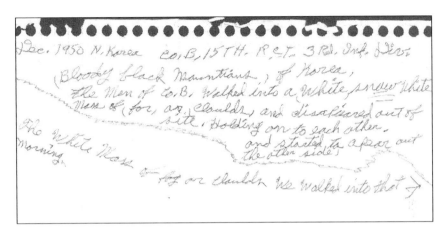

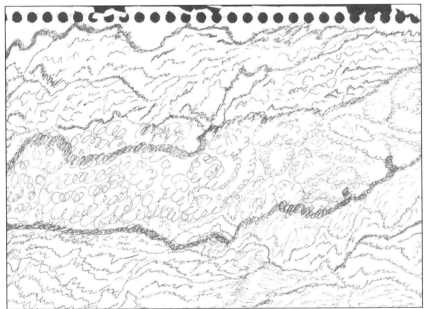

On his death bed, Bobby Grodhaus asked for a piece of paper. With ballpoint pen and his last breath, he drew the story of a fight we had during a snowstorm. He asked Shirley, his wife, to give it to me. Even when he was dying, Bobby thought about his wartime buddies. I treasure these thoughts of a dying hero.

SOLDIER

I WAS THAT WHICH OTHERS DID NOT WANT TO BE.

I WENT WHERE OTHERS FEARED TO GO, AND DID WHAT OTHERS FAILED TO DO.

I ASKED NOTHING FROM THOSE WHO GAVE NOTHING AND RELUCTANTLY ACCEPTED THE THOUGHT OF ETERNAL LONELINESS... SHOULD I FAIL.

I HAVE SEEN THE FACE OF TERROR, FELT THE STINGING COLD OF FEAR; AND ENJOYED THE SWEET TASTE OF A MOMENT'S LOVE.

I HAVE CRIED, PAINED, AND HOPED, BUT MOST OF ALL, I HAVE LIVED TIMES OTHERS WOULD SAY WERE BEST FORGOTTEN.

AT LEAST SOMEDAY I WILL BE ABLE TO SAY I WAS PROUD OF WHAT I WAS.....

A SOLDIER

Would I Do It Again?

I had the honor of serving my country.

I experienced the horrors of war, and because of combat, I have tinnitus (ringing in my ears from the loud noise of combat), frostbitten feet, nerve damage, shrapnel wounds, loss of full mobility of my legs, and PTSD.

Every day I walk around with the pains and ringing caused by combat, and upon reflection I ask the question, "Would I do it again?"

The answer is a resounding, "Yes!"

G.H. Chesterton said, "Courage is almost a contradiction in terms. It means a strong desire to live taking the form of a readiness to die." I was fortunate to experience true brotherhood where dying to save your buddy was not an option but understood; it was an integral part of our being. Words cannot explain the bond created among soldiers in combat. I marveled to be with men who were willing to die to save their buddies; men charging up a hill to certain death; men enduring bitter cold, lack of sleep, and, during all this time, never, I repeat never, slacking their duty. I was proud to serve my country and proud to have served with them.

**Memorial by foxhole buddy Herb Delventhal on Veterans Day in his yard.
It speaks volumes.**

After reading my story, my eldest daughter wrote this poem. It is indeed a proper end to my story.

WAR IS HELL

Dad Says War Is Hell
    Ringing Ears
    Cold Feet
    Tingling Toes and Nightmares
Any Regrets?
    Hell No! I'd Do It Again

— Debra Neumann

Purple Heart
Paragraph 2-8, Army Regulation 600-8-22 (Military Awards)
25 February 1995

The Purple Heart was established by General George Washington at Newburgh, New York, on 7 August 1782, during the Revolutionary War. It was reestablished by the President of the United States per War Department General Orders 3 in 1932 and is currently awarded pursuant to Executive Order 11016 (25 April 1962), Executive Order 12464 (23 February 1984), and Public Law 98-525 (19 October 1984).

The Purple Heart is awarded in the name of the President of the United States to any member of an Armed Force or any civilian national of the United States who, while serving under competent authority in any capacity with one of the US Armed Services after 5 April 1917, has been wounded or killed, or who has died or may hereafter die after being wounded in any action against an enemy of the United States.

Combat Infantry Badge

On November 21, 1950, I received the coveted Combat Infantry Badge. It is the most important award given to an infantryman. To earn it, a soldier must engage the enemy in the hostile fire area or in active ground combat involving an exchange of small arms fire at least five times. See the official order for issuing me the Combat Infantry Badge (CIB) below.

```
                    R-E-S-T-R-I-C-T-E-D

                       HEADQUARTERS
               15TH REGIMENTAL COMBAT TEAM
                       APO # 469
                 San Francisco, California

SPECIAL ORDERS                            21 November 1950
NUMBER   252

     2. UP of AR 600-70, the Combat Infantryman Badge is awarded to the follow-
ing-named officers and enlisted men of Co "B", 15th RCT for satisfactory perform-
ance of duty in ground combat against the enemy on 17 Nov 50:

     1ST LT       HAEGER, ARTHUR H.           0160311
     1ST LT       EDMUNDS, JAMES W.           0 .6331
     2D LT        MILLER, GEORGE A. JR.       0 2600
     2D LT        ROSS, JERRY R.              0  91
     WOJG         CANNON, MALCOLM F.          RW 241217
     M/SGT        KING, WILLIAM M.            RA36 734 046
     M/SGT        JOHNSON, DANIEL E.          RA
     SFC          ARCHER, RICHARD E.          RA13     412
     SFC          KING, HORACE L.             RA4  4 1 197
     SFC          BROUGHN, GEORGE F.          RA11 017
     SFC          FRAZIER, DONALD G.          RA16 212 272
     SFC          HARRISON, CLARENCE R.       RA34 935 3 1
     SFC          HAYES, CHARLIS              RA 6 386 251
     SFC          LLOYD, JAMES O. JR.         RA39 473 309
     SFC          SPRADLIN, EUGENE R.         RA 3 512 548
     SFC          SUMPTION, DALE N.           RA55 412 101
     SFC          TAILOR, DUARD E.            RA16 222 750
     SGT          BONNER, HENRY E.
     PVT          API, DAVID G.               RA13 351 317
     PVT          AXE, FRANKLIN P.            RA13 344 965
     PVT          KAKAZU, SUEO                RA10 104 501
     PVT          KOGA, MELVIN F.             RA10 104 499
     PVT          LIPTKE, ALEXANDER K. JR.    RA10 104 495
     PVT          LEE, ENOCH                  RA10 104 459
     PVT          NIELSON, WESLEY D.          ER55 009 232
     PVT          MUNOZ, BERNARD G.           EA19 257 234
     PVT          PETTINGER, HARVIN J.        ER55 009 348
     PVT          TOMKINS, PHILLIP A.         ER55 009 270
     PVT          TRACEY, ALLEN W.            RA27 910 177
     PVT          SHERMAN, ROLAND K.          RA17 280 760
     PVT          ROHRBACK, LAWRENCE N. JR.   RA23 303 166
     PVT          ROBERS, ARTHUR C.           RA19 361 285
     PVT          CANDELARIA, PEDRO           RA18 366 990
     PVT          SEYMORE, JOHN W.            RA13 337 238
     PVT          SHIVES, PAUL F.             RA13 343 092
     PVT          SHIRTS, WILLARD E.          RA16 330 554
     PVT          SMITH, CHARLES E.           RA13 348 578
     PVT          SONSALLA, DONALD R.         RA16 329 321
     PVT          SPANBAUER, ROBERT R.        RA15 424 938
     PVT          MC-LEVIS, WILLIAM F.        ER17 217 368
     PVT          GRODHAUS, ROBERT F.         RA15 424 894
     PVT          HICKOX, EVERETT D. JR.      RA19 368 840
     PVT          HILBURGER, HARRY S.         RA16 310 183
     PVT          HUDSON, GERALD L.           RA16 310 168
```

A Copy of DD 214, My Official Record of Service

List of medals earned: Korean Service Ribbon (combat in Korea), four Bronze Stars (for heroic actions), UN Ribbon (fighting with UN troops), Purple Heart (wounded in action), Combat Infantry Badge (under fire by the enemy), and two Overseas Bars (for 1950 and 1951 action).

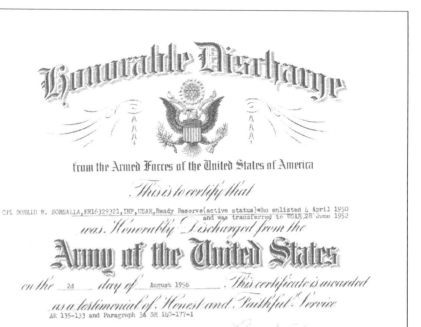

Donald R. Sonsalla, PhD, proud of his service
to his country.

IN APPRECIATION

I deeply appreciate, more than words can say, the understanding my lovely wife, Verna, has shown over the years living with my night terrors/nightmares (now known as Post-traumatic Stress Disorder or PTSD). This has not been easy, and I am extremely grateful for her love and support.

THANK YOU

I want to thank my friends and family who previewed a rough draft of my book and offered suggestions. A thank you also goes to my daughters Judy and Debra; my wife, Verna; and Sherry Roberts, of The Roberts Group, who helped edit as I continually rewrote and edited this book. Finally, I hope we ended up with a story that will help the reader understand the complexity of combat and the realities of war.

57280908R00088

Made in the USA
Lexington, KY
10 November 2016